Wyandotte: A Pictorial History
The Early Years

Wyandotte: *A Pictorial History*
The Early Years

Published by

WYANDOTTE HISTORICAL SOCIETY

1997

Copyright 1997
by the
Wyandotte Historical Society
Wyandotte, Michigan

Library of Congress Number

97-077664

ISBN 0-8187-0309-1

INTRODUCTION

This publication is intended to be an entertaining photo album of our community—Wyandotte, Michigan. It is not intended as a comprehensive history of our city. That effort has been ably accomplished by Edwina DeWindt in her two publications, *Proudly We Record* and *Our Fame and Fortune in Wyandotte*. The book proceeds in a loose chronological order from the earliest times of the founding of our city and into the 1930's. Its content and emphasis were largely determined by the photographs available.

The people who peer out at us from these photographs of long ago were far more like ourselves than different. Each of us, past and present, has been given this place called "Wyandotte" in which to live our lives. Each generation has the opportunity to appreciate and renew our city. By seeing what came before, we gain a deeper appreciation of Wyandotte, and a renewed dedication to invest in its future.

ACKNOWLEDGMENTS

We wish to express our deep gratitude to Edwina DeWindt for her past writings on Wyandotte history. Her works were a source of much of the information used in this publication. Thanks also go to Barbara Wallace, Director of the Bacon Memorial District Library, and to Marc Partin, Supervisor of Wyandotte Museums, for providing access to thousands of historical photographs. Furthermore, we thank the Bacon Memorial District Library for use of its facilities in the production of this work. We are most grateful to the Wyandotte Historical Society for funding and publishing this book. We also appreciate the comments and suggestions of Valerie Brighton, David Fox, Beth Kowaleski, Alex Leskiw and Joyce Schroeder.

This book was researched, compiled and written by the members of the Publications Committee of the Wyandotte Historical Society who labored faithfully for several years on the project. The Committee sadly notes the passing of Robert Schroeder as the publication was going to press.

THE COMMITTEE
Wallace Hayden, Chairman
George Gouth   Yvonne Latta
Kenneth Navarre   Robert Schroeder
Nancy Wesser

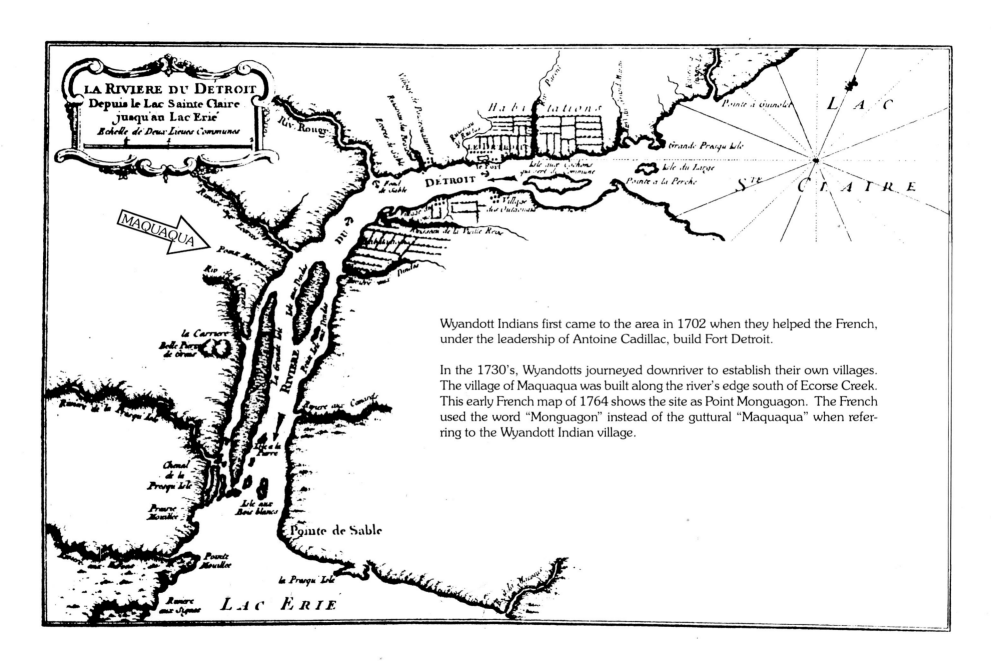

MAQUAQUA

LA RIVIERE DU DETROIT
Depuis le Lac Sainte Claire
jusqu'au Lac Erié
Echelle de Deux Lieues Communes

Wyandott Indians first came to the area in 1702 when they helped the French, under the leadership of Antoine Cadillac, build Fort Detroit.

In the 1730's, Wyandotts journeyed downriver to establish their own villages. The village of Maquaqua was built along the river's edge south of Ecorse Creek. This early French map of 1764 shows the site as Point Monguagon. The French used the word "Monguagon" instead of the guttural "Maquaqua" when referring to the Wyandott Indian village.

Indian Village of Maquaqua

The early years of the Wyandotts were peaceful. Their French allies were nearby and food was plentiful. The Wyandotts (called "Huron" by the French) had accepted Christianity, and reestablished themselves as fur merchants.

In 1760, Maquaqua came under British rule when the British defeated the French in Canada and immediately took over Fort Detroit.

By 1796, Fort Detroit and the area along the river were governed by Americans. The Wyandotts of Maquaqua had lived under three flags.

The 1818 Treaty of St. Mary's moved the Wyandotts from Maquaqua to a nearby site in Huron Township. In 1842, those Wyandotts and others from Ohio were moved to Kansas.

Major John Biddle
1792-1859

John Biddle came to the area during the War of 1812 while serving in the military. After the war he purchased 2200 acres of land along the Detroit River, which included the Village of Maquaqua. A family estate was built on the present site of the MacNichol home.

Major Biddle named his estate "Wyandotte" after the Indians who lived on the site. John Biddle sold his lands to Eber Ward in 1853. The mansion was used as a carriage stop until a fire destroyed most of the home in 1860.

Our city honored this pioneer by naming the main thoroughfare Biddle Avenue.

The original plat of Wyandotte extended from Third Street to the river and from Orchard to Walnut Street. By 1896, the village had expanded to the railroad tracks. The acreage west of the tracks would become known as Glenwood.

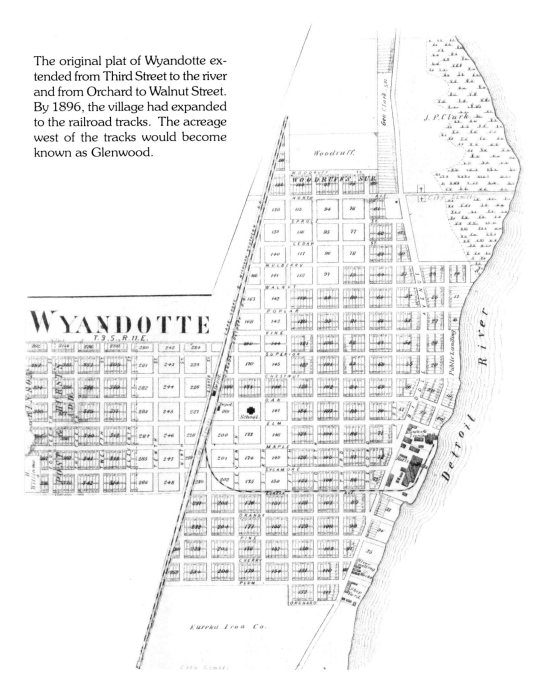

Captain Eber Brock Ward
1811-1875

Captain Eber Ward was the industrialist and financier who helped forge the Industrial Revolution in the United States. In 1853, he founded the Eureka Iron Company and the following year platted the Village of Wyandotte. He reserved the waterfront for his iron manufacturing facilities and his other companies, silver smelting and shipbuilding.

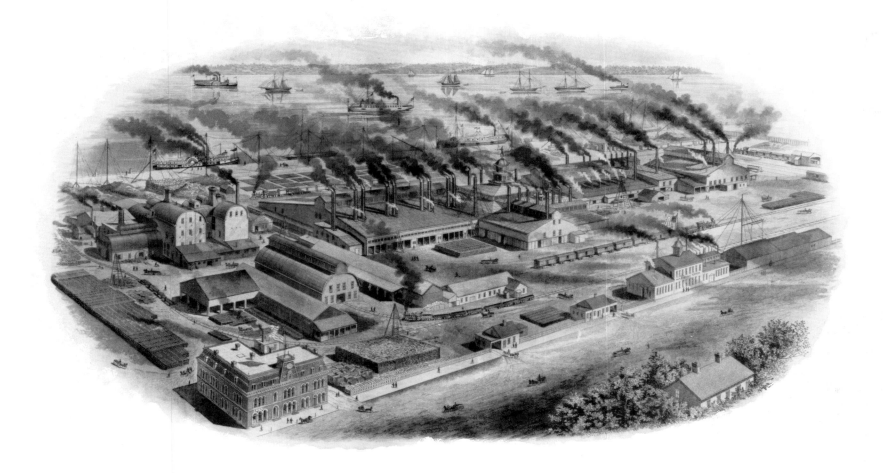

EUREKA IRON CO.

DETROIT, MICHIGAN.

Mills & Furnaces,
WYANDOTTE,
MICH.

General Offices,
DETROIT,
MICH.

The Eureka Iron Company was the major industry (1854-1892) along the Detroit River in the budding Village of Wyandotte. Irish and German workers were recruited from New Jersey and New York. The industry flourished and Wyandotte grew into a major manufacturing center. Rolling mills and shipyards were added, and "Wyandotte" iron rails, boiler plate, pig iron, iron bar and iron-hulled ships became known throughout the United States.

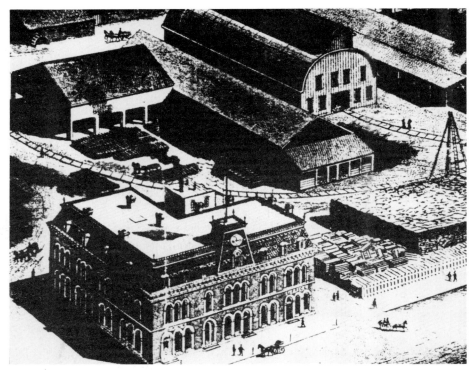

At peak production, over 6000 cords of charcoal were consumed each day to smelt the iron ore that was shipped in from Lake Superior mines. Billowing smoke spewed from the countless stacks of the Eureka Iron Company. The office building at 3005 Biddle is the last remaining evidence of the days when "Iron was King" in Wyandotte. The historic plaque at Elm and Van Alstyne recalls the year 1864 when the nation's first steel was made with the Kelly Converter at the Iron Works.

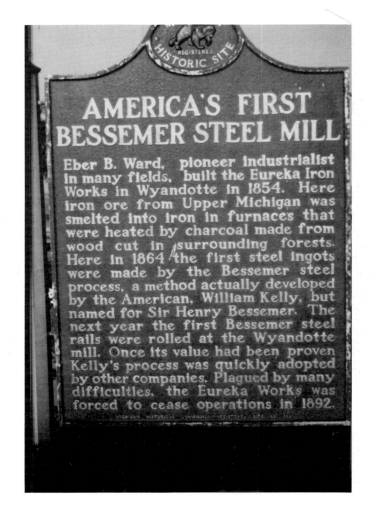

AMERICA'S FIRST BESSEMER STEEL MILL

Eber B. Ward, pioneer industrialist in many fields, built the Eureka Iron Works in Wyandotte in 1854. Here iron ore from Upper Michigan was smelted into iron in furnaces that were heated by charcoal made from wood cut in surrounding forests. Here in 1864 the first steel ingots were made by the Bessemer steel process, a method actually developed by the American, William Kelly, but named for Sir Henry Bessemer. The next year the first Bessemer steel rails were rolled at the Wyandotte mill. Once its value had been proven Kelly's process was quickly adopted by other companies. Plagued by many difficulties, the Eureka Works was forced to cease operations in 1892.

John M. Bryan (1833-1903)

A Civil War veteran who traveled to Wyandotte to work at the Rolling Mills, John Bryan was appointed lighthouse keeper at Grassy Island. His sons Edward and William went on to distinguish themselves in politics & business.

The village of Wyandotte was involved in the Civil War. Troops were on guard at the Eureka Iron Works to protect against possible sabotage by Southern sympathizers.

The Iron Works production of rail, bar iron and boiler plate was used in the war effort. In addition, Michigan's 24th "Iron Brigade" included 23 Wyandotters. The hard-fighting unit was tested in over 20 major battles and 1000 skirmishes, including Gettysburg, Fredericksburg, Chancellorsville and the Wilderness.

Three Wyandotte men were killed in the war, Asa Brindle (nephew of Eber Ward), Lewis Baldwin and George Pinkney. Wyandotte's two cemeteries have numerous headstones attesting to the city's involvement during the Civil War.

Company House 1864

Company houses were built for the Eureka Iron Works employees. Later, two-story "rolling mill" houses were also built.

Marx House 1874

This was the home of William Marx, son of George Marx who, in 1863, established the Marx Brewing Company. The home is on the northeast corner of Oak and Third Streets.

Armstrong House 1856

The William Armstrong family lived here from 1870 to the early 1900's. The George Marx family purchased the home in 1921. Wyandotte's oldest brick home is listed on the State's historical register as the Marx House.

J. S. Van Alstyne House 1870

Originally located on Biddle near Superior, the J. S. Van Alstyne Home was Wyandotte's first house with a bay window. In 1902, the building was moved to Van Alstyne between Maple and Sycamore. John Van Alstyne was the city's first mayor.

The First Presbyterian Church was organized in 1856. The old Brown School served the congregation as a meeting place until they built their own church at Chestnut and First in 1900. It served the Presbyterians until 1962 when a new church was built at Oak and 23rd Streets.

First Presbyterian Church

St. Johns Evangelical Church

St. John United Church of Christ, originally known as St. John German Evangelical Church, was organized in 1870. The cornerstone was laid in 1871, and the church was dedicated the following year.

Trinity Lutheran Church 1888

The German Lutherans of Wyandotte organized their own church and school in 1861. The tall spired building at Oak and Fifth became known as Trinity Lutheran Church. After 100 years, the New England styled church was razed and a modern edifice was built on the same site.

St. Stephens Episcopal Church

The Episcopalians started a mission church in 1859. The first St. Stephen's, built at the corner of First and Chestnut, was razed in 1964 and a new church was built on the same site.

These young pupils of the "Old Brown School" went on to become the pioneer families of Wyandotte who kept alive memories of slate boards and hickory sticks. A favorite teacher was Ida Johnson Nixon, shown front row center with the Hurst twins, Eva and Effie, seated on either side of her.

Wyandotte's first temple of learning was the First Ward School. The one-room school was built on Chestnut Street, just west of Biddle Avenue, donated by the Eureka Iron Company.

The building served as a school from 1856 to 1887. In the years that followed, the "Old Brown School" was used as a council hall, an Opera House, and a meeting place for various churches and civic organizations.

In 1910, the structure was moved to Third Street and made into two apartments (2035 & 2043 Third). The present Masonic Temple building (81 Chestnut) stands on the original site of the First Ward School.

18

Houses, schools, churches and small businesses were needed by the workers and their families. The essentials of a village naturally developed around the Iron Works. The census of 1869 registered 1700 inhabitants. In this photo, Aaron Strong is shown on the left. On the right, Joseph Girardin, Sr., William Girardin, Mrs. Joseph Girardin, Sr. and family friend Lena Gee enjoy a summer day from the front porch. Tragedy would befall at least two in this photo. Lena Gee would die just days before her wedding day, and be buried in her gown. Many years later, Aaron Strong would be electrocuted while painting the interior of the dynamo room at the municipal power plant.

Starting as Genthe & Girardin Groceries, each man eventually had his own store. Wooden sidewalks were in evidence. Flour was locally produced at the T. C. Gray Flour Mill located at the corner of Van Alstyne and Oak.

When Charles Thomas opened Wyandotte's first drug store
on the west side of Biddle Avenue between Oak and Elm
Streets, it also served as a first aid station. This business
existed from 1863 to 1923, and then became a Woolworth
dime store. Note the wooden sidewalks, wooden interior
floors, and large cigar display.

In 1888, Charles E. Kreger wanted to move to the "Big Town," so he sold his grocery stock in Taylor Center and moved to the corner of Pine and Biddle in Wyandotte.

The first volunteer fire department was formed in 1870. In 1876, the first fire engine was purchased. This picture from the late 1870's shows an early engine at Biddle and Elm.

In 1871, a group headed by John S. Van Alstyne and Captain Eber Ward organized the Wyandotte Savings Bank. The first quarters of the Bank were in the office building of the Eureka Iron Company. The building served the needs of both firms until the Eureka Iron Company went out of business. During its centennial celebration, it was recognized as probably the only bank in Michigan to have been in the same building for 100 years.

J. S. VAN ALSTYNE
WYANDOTTE
PRESIDENT WYANDOTTE SAVINGS BANK

John S. Van Alstyne (third from the left) is pictured in front of the Wyandotte Savings Bank. Mr. Van Alstyne, the bank's first president, played many important roles in early Wyandotte. He managed the first sales of land in the new village, managed the Eureka Iron Works, served as the city's first mayor in 1867, and founded the local Masonic Lodge.

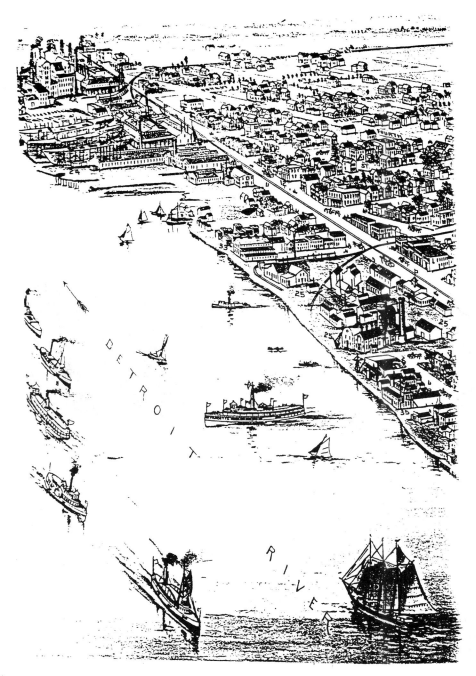

In the 1850's, the Detroit River served as a major highway bringing settlers and materials to the fledgling village. Many industries established factories and warehouses along its banks.

For residents, too, the river provided much in the way of necessity and recreation, including drinking water, ice, fishing, boating, ice skating and a cool swim on a hot summer's day.

Grassy Island lighthouse, was built in 1849 and refitted in 1867. John Bryan was the keeper, and lived there with his wife and four children.

This is a photograph of one of the Clark family fisheries along the Detroit River. John Clark brought his family to Manguagon (Wyandotte) in 1818. His son George bought Grassy Island in 1833 and fished from Belle Isle to Maumee, Ohio. In those days the waters off Wyandotte were filled with whitefish.

Captain Eber Ward added a new industry to Wyandotte's riverfront in 1871. Shipyards were built south of Eureka along the river's edge. The renowned Kirby brothers, Frank E. and Fitzhugh (Joe), were commissioned by Eber Ward to operate the yards and design ships. Over the next fifty years more than 200 hulls would be launched from the Wyandotte works.

Frank Kirby designed the ships at the Wyandotte yards. He was both an architect and engineer. Henry Ford inscribed his name second under Thomas Edison on the memorial arch at Greenfield Village as an outstanding American Genius.

The *Frank E. Kirby* was launched in 1890. Named in honor of the renowned marine architect, the side wheeler ran the route to Put-In-Bay for 30 years.

Many newspaper items of the time were folksy, like this one from the *Wyandotte Herald* of August 12, 1892:

Baby Frank C. Kirby, F. A. Kirby's youngest, was asked last Sunday what was sung in Sunday school. His answer was "Wyandotte for Jesus." Upon further inquiry it was learned that the song was "Why not for Jesus."

Hulls were constructed at the Wyandotte plant, then towed to Detroit for completion.

Launchings were festive occasions. Children were let out of school and crowds cheered as the ships slid sideways down the ways and into the river with a mighty splash.

Activity reached a peak during World War I. Between 1917 and 1919, seventy-seven ships were built for the war effort and the Merchant Marines.

The D. H. Burrell Hoop & Stave Company was established in 1885 by the riverfront between Walnut and Mulberry. About 125 men worked in four mills making cheese boxes and hoops and staves for barrels and kegs.

The Herald Edition of May 31, 1889 stated:
The engineer at D. H. Burrell & Co. blew the whistle so hard yesterday afternoon that the people in the first ward thought the factory was on fire, and Engineer Finn started to get out the fire department.

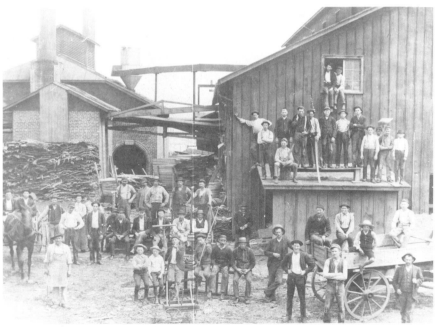

Workers gathered in front of the south plant boiler room, about 1890.

Burrell managers John Nellis, Ed Hunter, R. B. Burrell, N. N. Fairchild and Clifford Burrell are pictured in front of the office.

Logs were either hauled in from nearby farms or floated down the river. By 1902, the local supply of lumber had been depleted and the business closed. Note the salt wells of the Michigan Alkali plant in the background of the picture below.

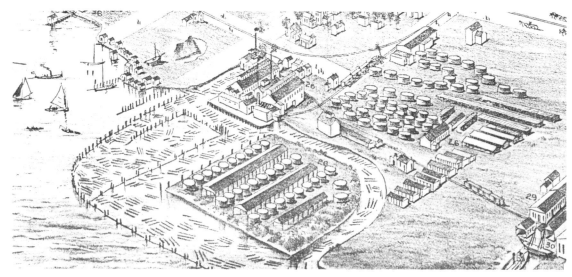

An 1896 bird's eye sketch of the Burrell Company, shows the storage areas around Bark Island in the foreground. Later the Wyandotte General Hospital and a marina would occupy the site.

The crew of the north plant assembles for a photograph, about 1895.

Many smaller, independent ship builders operated in the shadow of the Burrell Company. Edward and William Bryan were most notable. The Bryan Boat Works stood on Mulberry near the river. From 1908 to 1951, the brothers built many small craft and pleasure boats.

Edward C. Bryan, pictured above in 1901, distinguished himself in more than just boat building. He was an artistic painter, City Clerk, Commissioner, and member of the Michigan House of Representatives.

William F. and Edward C. Bryan preferred using hand tools as much as possible.

In 1863, George Marx founded the City Brewery, later called the Marx Brewery, on the river at the foot of Oak Street. In its first year, the brewery had an annual capacity of 1000 barrels, but expanded to 100,000 barrels and could bottle 6000 pints per hour. National prohibition put an end to alcohol production. From 1926 to 1928, the brewery was used to manufacture the Hess aircraft.

Marx Employees
Top row, left to right: Adam Pierson, Andrew Hock, Chris Thon, Charles Springstead, Billie Benjamin, Nick Megges. Middle row: Joe Marx, William Marx, Ferdinand Fickel, Jack Berndt. Boy: Frank Stephanie.

An early photo of the Marx Brewery horse-drawn delivery wagons on Oak at the river.

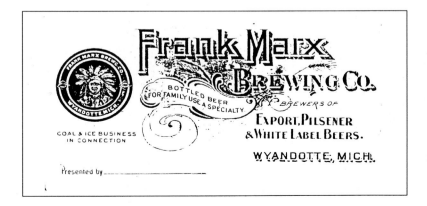

An 1891 newspaper item noted that a Wyandotte man was arrested for passing a confederate $5 bill in a saloon.

Jerome Holland Bishop was one of Wyandotte's most influential and generous citizens. His leadership began in 1871, when he assumed the Superintendency of the city's public schools. In 1875, Mr. Bishop resigned and established the J. H. Bishop Fur Company. Recognized as an outstanding businessman and civic leader, he was elected to five terms as Mayor.

J. H. Bishop is also remembered for his philanthropic works that included assisting most early churches, building the First Congregational Church, providing land for a park, funding the public library, and offering his home for use as a City Hall.

Jerome Holland Bishop (1846-1928)

The employees at the Bishop Fur Company held the highest respect for J. H. Bishop (shown holding his derby at far right). In the 40 years of the company's existence in Wyandotte, there was never a labor conflict or strike.

The Bishop Fur Company grew along the waterfront on Front Street between Oak and Chestnut. Well over one hundred Wyandotters found employment at the "Tannery" as it was referred to in the early days. Wool dusters, robes, coats, gloves and rugs were manufactured at the Wyandotte site. World War I stopped the trade in furs from foreign sources, so the company was forced to close. The buildings were demolished and the land sold to the city for a modest price. Today we know this site as Bishop Park.

Founded in 1880, The River Park Hotel was located on the waterfront between Poplar and Walnut. It was an elegant health resort which boasted that its mineral spring baths, recreational activities, excellent meals, relaxing green lawns, river breezes and veranda were a certain cure for everything from nervous disorders, to the effects of youthful indiscretions, to paralysis. The building burned in 1889.

The reputation of the hotel spread beyond the local area. Many people, including some famous ones, arrived by train or side-wheeler steamers at the resort's own dock.

Even some of the locals enjoyed the hotel's amenities.

Biddle Avenue is one of the oldest roads in the State of Michigan. It was constructed during the war of 1812 by soldiers under General Hull and follows an early trail to the River Raisin. It was then called "The Military Road."

Biddle Avenue, 1890, between Elm and Oak

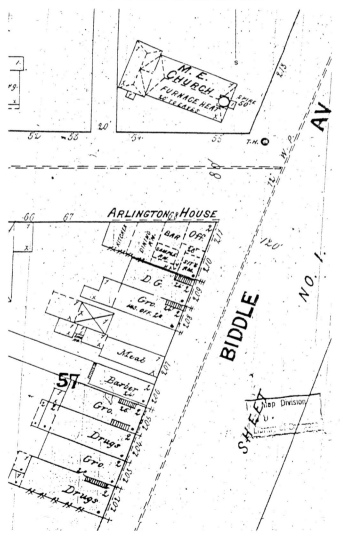

With the establishment of the city of Wyandotte, Biddle Avenue attracted not only a business district, but many stately homes as well. This is the J. B. Ford, Jr. residence on the northwest corner of Superior and Biddle.

Social life revolved around the churches which organized picnics, boating and parades. Civic organizations such as the Tuesday Study Club explored community problems and needs. Schools held graduations and offered adult education. Politics guided the business of the growing village, and the Marx Opera House booked Chautauqua lectures and theatre groups.

St. Joseph Church Choir, 1880
Standing in the back row are Rose Sanger, Kate Brohl, Joe Hoersch, Catherine Otto, John George and Emma Otto. The two young men seated in chairs are Ed George, on the left, and Peter Mauren. In the front row are Elizabeth Tillman, Frank George, Henrietta Brohl and Mary Otto.

Many of the old neighborhoods looked very much like today. Here is the Charles Sanders house at 325 Poplar, about 1915. The three children at the left are May Adair, Lavonne Schultz and Margaret Adair. Seated on the steps is Matilda Mae Sanders.

Located on the southwest corner of Biddle and Oak, The Arlington Hotel was noted for its fine food, excellent liquor and lavish furnishings. J. P. Debo was an early proprietor. Others in this photograph are J. P. Loselle, John L. Correyell, G. F. Giasson, N. A. Roberts and H. D. Gilson. The hotel operated from 1884 to 1919. In 1920, the building was leased by Frank Armstrong for use as a men's clothing store.

From The Wyandotte News Herald
September 27, 1895
"Joe Hoersch, the accommodating clerk at the Arlington house, who has been losing flesh telling people when the next car was due on the electric road, has invented a scheme to regain his avoirdupois. He has made a contrivance in the form of a clock dial which tells on the face of it when the next car is due and in which direction it will go. Joe has a big club lying handy now, and the next man who inquires about street cars will furnish a subject for a coroner's jury."

Tillie Hoersch stands in the doorway of the Hoersch Shoe Store which she operated. At the left are the inning-by-inning baseball scores of interest.

C. F. Smith Company Pure Food Stores, at 2954 Biddle Avenue, shows a typical store layout where customers presented their grocery lists and then waited while the store clerk gathered the items for packaging.

This jewelry and optical business was located next to the Majestic Theatre. Note the chandelier, eye chart, stove and floor vault...all items that are not likely to be seen in the customer area of today's businesses.

JOSEPH GIRARDIN & SON,
Manufacturers and Dealers In
CARRIAGES, WAGONS
—AND—
IRON WHEELBARROWS
WYANDOTTE, MICH.

Pictured in front of the Girardin Carriage and Wagon Shop, about 1890, are Aaron Strong, Lee Miller, Alfred Kreger, Warren Girardin and an unknown child.

Brohl's Bakery was originally located on the west side of Biddle Avenue at the corner of Elm Street. Pictured, about 1868, are Joseph and Francis Brohl along with Charles George.

Hugo Mehlhose started a confectionery in 1875 on the west side of Biddle Avenue between Oak and Elm Streets. Both Hugo Mehlhose and Fred Sanders claimed to be the first person to serve ice cream sodas. The two agreed to share the invention. The Mehlhose ice cream factory began operation on Fourth Street in 1888.

The Niagara Laundry was located at the northwest corner of Oak and First Streets as well as at an earlier Biddle Avenue address. Oscar Stieler, its proprietor, also owned the White Swan Steam Laundry at the foot of Oak Street.

August Loeffler founded A. Loeffler Clothing in 1881 on the west side of Biddle Avenue between Eureka and Sycamore. The store's name was changed to A. Loeffler & Co. in 1905 when William Thon and William Mehlhose became partners. By 1935, theirs was the largest store between Toledo and Detroit. It was a sad day for everyone when the business closed in January 1939.

In July 1883, the City contracted to purchase 50 oil street lamps for $600 (25 on Biddle, 14 on Oak, 8 on Eureka and 3 on Elm) and hired a man to light and tend the lamps. By 1889, one alderman complained that "the lamp lighter don't light the lamps when the moon shines." In June the lamp lighter was hauled over the coals and admonished to keep his oil lights trimmed and burning in good shape.

Wyandotte Electric Light Company began furnishing electric illumination for the City in December of 1889. To celebrate the occasion, the Excelsior Band played beneath the different lights on Biddle Avenue. A. Loeffler Clothing was one of the first stores to install electricity.

James "Dolly" Haven established his printing business in 1879. The presses were powered by a neighboring business, Gray's Flour Mill. The first Wyandotte Herald Newspaper was printed in his shop. From 1886 to his death in 1943, Dolly Haven was editor of the newspaper. His son continued the printing business as J. D. Haven and Son.

James D. Haven photographed as a young child with his mother.

Pedestrians stroll on Biddle Avenue near the intersection of First Street. The banner strung across Biddle indicates that a Chautauqua is coming to town.

Poised to clearly show the Melody Brothers sign on its Biddle building, this horse and wagon stand at attention. Also notable in the background is the fire station tower, at Elm and First Streets, in which the fire hoses were hung to drain. Established in 1895, Melody's was one of the first to apply for incandescent lamps from the city lighting plant.

The interior of the Girardin Grocery shows a well stocked store. Notice the gas lamp hanging overhead. A baby buggy is on the right.

Theodore Megges served as City Alderman in 1876, but was perhaps better known for his billiard hall and sample room on Biddle Avenue. Eureka Lager Beer signs promoted the City's own Eureka Brewery which was located in what is now the northern end of Bishop Park.

The Kaul brothers, John, Henry and William started their department store in 1880 on the west side of Biddle between Eureka and Sycamore. In 1888, this store had the distinction of having the first stone sidewalk. Kaul's remained in operation until the 1980's.

Established in 1879 as a general store, Cahalan's became a drug store one year later. It also served as a first aid station to the Eureka Iron and Steel Company employees. The business operated in three different locations between Oak and Elm.

The **Bishop Chemical Co.** Ltd.

Sole Proprietors of

Cahalan's Curo-Baldo and Cahalan's
Curo=Baldo Soap.

J. K. Bishop, Pres.
Jno. C. Cahalan, Sec'y.
Richard E. Cahalan, Treas.
Jno. F. McInerney, Mgr.

Wyandotte, Mich.,

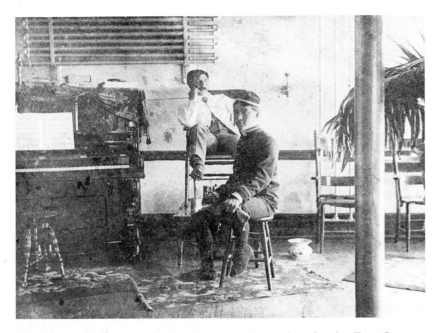

The Wiseman Brothers Barber Shop was located under the First Commercial and Savings Bank at Biddle and Oak. In this 1898 photo, the bootblack seated on the stool is the young Everett Payette. The spittoon on the floor in the background was a vital part of the decor of the day.

Joseph Girardin, Sr. gets a trim from barber Julius Thiede in 1890.

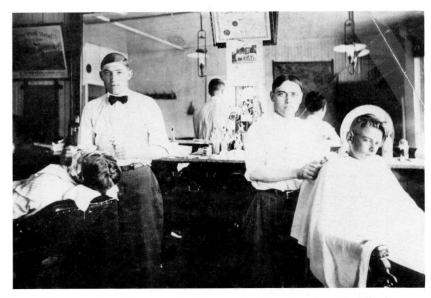

Later, Everette Payette opened his own barber shop on Biddle between Northline and Sullivan. Mr. Payette is the barber on the right.

Charles McColl, M. D. pauses at the corner of Chestnut and First Streets in 1898. St. Patrick Church is the building in the background. Typically, doctors charged $1 for house calls and 50 cents for office visits.

It was not uncommon for local businessmen to gather for a formal portrait. Sitting are Joseph Girardin, Jr. and Conrad Genthe. Behind them are Charles Thomas II, Henry Weatherwax, Tony Roehrig and Fred Johnson.

August Tacke made regular deliveries from his meat market on Sycamore Street. He served as an Alderman of the Second Ward in 1893 and 1895.

In 1891, the Union Railway depot was completed at a cost of $14,000. Over one hundred years later, the building still stands between the tracks at Oak Street.

During the 1890's, the railroads offered the most reliable and extensive year-round transportation. Twenty passenger trains stopped daily at the Oak Street station.

The first station in 1855 was a box car. It was later replaced by this wooden structure.

The railroad first came to the city in 1855 in the form of the Detroit, Monroe, Toledo Railroad (later the New York Central System). Several others were added over the next 50 years, including the Michigan Central.

Alexander Gee and Roy Paine look out from the railroad switching tower in 1891.

Other early railroad names to run through Wyandotte included the Toledo Shoreline, the Detroit and Lima Northern and the Detroit, Toledo and Ironton.

On October 14, 1880, the city passed an ordinance prohibiting boys from jumping on and off of cars and locomotives.

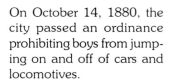

A train crew poses in front of a Michigan Central switch engine in the 1890's.

Ladies Euchre Club

It was not uncommon to have a group of friends pose for a formal portrait such as this one taken in 1890. From the top, left to right are: Mae Girardin, Myrtle Kirby, Hessie Andrews, Nettie Hathaway, Mae Bolton, Laura Watkins, Hattie Smith, Joda Haines, Grace Clark and Emily Pray.

This gathering gives us an especially
good look at the fashions of the day.
Members of the Daffodil Club included
many familiar names such as Christian,
Van Alstyne, Burrell, Pray, Lacy, Bishop
and Clark.

Friends gather in the Fairchild's dining room
in 1895. Lottie Fairchild stands just to the
right of the wall phone. Others in the group
include such names as Girardin, Stiles,
Babcock, Davis, Malcolm, Haas, Woodruff
and Clark.

The first houses in the village were constructed for the work-men of the Eureka Iron Works, mostly from Oak Street, south to Pine. They were one floor, meager dwellings. By 1870, the city had developed a class of managers, merchants and professionals who built larger, more substantial homes, mostly from Oak Street north.

James Campbell's home was on the north side of Chestnut between First and Second Streets. Mr. Campbell was mayor in 1877. Note the boardwalk and muddy street.

The Mehlhose family immigrated from Germany in the 1860's. Louis Mehlhose built this house around 1865. His brother Hugo, pictured above, was one of the earliest ice cream makers in this area.

In 1891, a newspaper item told that:
"Mayor Campbell has purchased a bicycle—the only one in town-and is now practicing daily in the mold loft at the shipyard before making his debut."

Within a few years, a bicycle path was designated down Biddle Avenue next to the streetcar tracks.

In 1856, Eby's General Dry Goods opened at Biddle and Elm, and was possibly the first store building in Wyandotte. Henry Eby served as Village Postmaster from 1856 to 1864. His home was located on Biddle near Vinewood.

Henry Eby House 1880-90

Owner of a boot and shoe store, Henry Roehrig served in the 1890's as Postmaster, Treasurer and Mayor. His home on Biddle between Vinewood and Poplar was occupied by the Wabeek Dining Room from 1939-96.

Henry Roehrig House 1888

Girardin House 1892

Anna Asbahr's parents lived in this home, and her father was an early Councilman. She and her husband, Henry Girardin, later occupied the home until it was razed for urban renewal. Anna Asbahr Girardin is remembered for being the first person to offer her private papers of Wyandotte history to the Bacon Memorial Library.

W. C. Lambert House 1896

Walter C. Lambert, M. D. opened a Biddle Avenue office in 1886, but later moved it to his home on Biddle between Chestnut and Superior. He helped organize the Wyandotte Sanitarium, the Emergency Hospital, and served as Chief of Staff at Wyandotte General Hospital when it opened in 1926. He also served as Mayor.

High School Class of 1899

Jerome Holland Bishop was Superintendent of Schools in 1875 when the first graduating class of "Old Central" was honored in the Bank Hall. Five girls were in the class. The new 2nd Ward School had separate entrances for boys and girls, six classrooms, and seated 340 students. A high school education was a very noble accomplishment and early graduation classed were small. The class of 1899 had only ten graduates, including pioneer family names of Clark, Thon, Drennan and Loeffler. From 1875 to 1885 inclusive, only fifty-eight students earned their diplomas.

The city's first high school was built in 1869 on Oak Street east of the railroad tracks. The school was in operation until 1905.

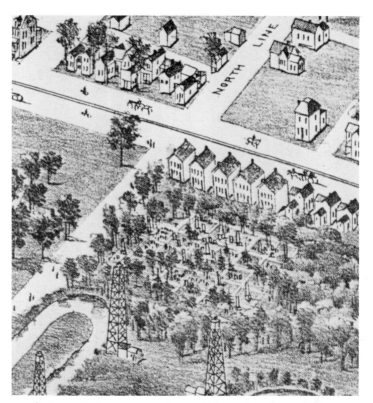

For the first decade of its existence, Wyandotte did not have its own cemetery. In 1865, nine acres of land were set aside at Northline and Ninth Street to become Mt. Carmel Cemetery. It was used primarily for Catholic families and is still being used for burials.

Oakwood Cemetery is located near the Detroit River on Northline Road just east of Biddle Avenue on land originally used as part of the John Clark farm. The first burials were John Clark and his eleven year old daughter, both of whom died in the early 1800's. The property did not become recognized as a cemetery until 1869. An addition was added in 1892. Many of Wyandotte's early pioneers were buried there, including mayors, doctors, attorneys, business leaders and veterans of the Civil War and Spanish-American War.

Henry Thon's hearse is at the ready for a funeral procession in front of the First Methodist Church on Biddle Avenue and Oak Street. The Presbyterian Church at Chestnut Street is on the right and the Old Brown School is behind. Note the new streetcar tracks in this photo from about 1895.

The first undertaking service in the village of Wyandotte was established by J. F. W. Thon in 1857. Mr. Thon, a carpenter by trade, made caskets tapered in the shape of the human body. In 1865, his son Henry (pictured above) joined the business as did another son, Christian, in later years.

For many years, they were located at Sycamore and Biddle, but moved to the corner of Chestnut and Biddle in 1935.

J.F.W. Thon also built many of the early buildings in town, including the Eureka Iron Works offices, the Old Brown School, St. John's Church and many homes.

From the Wyandotte Herald
Friday, August 14, 1891

PHONES { 7 J Store
7 J J Kings, House
Sunday and Night Call

Wyandotte, Mich., *Feby. 10th* 191*7*

BOUGHT OF

HENRY F. THON

UNDERTAKER

AND DEALER IN FURNITURE

No. 23-25 Biddle Ave.

Jany 30	To Casket & Box		95	
"	Embalming		7	
"	Auto Hearse		10	
"	1 Auto		5	
"	5 Autos @ 4.		20	
"	Palms		2	50
"	Sexton		7	
"	Hearse & Grave Trimming		3	
"	Candles		1	25
"	Wreath on Door		2	
"	Gloves		1	50
"	Chairs		1	00
"	Digging grave		5	
			160	25

Paid in full 8/17/17 H. F. Thon

This photo of city officials of 1888 contains some of the more easily recognizable names in Wyandotte history including Lacy, Marx, Bigler, Langlois and Genthe.

After complaints of poor workmanship, fighting among contractors and work delays, the new city hall was finished in 1881. The first floor housed the fire department and jail. The second floor was a public hall.

This pedestrian's eye view of Biddle and Elm looks west toward City Hall.

A fire wagon sits outside the new fire station.

This is another photo of the same wagon with a crew of firefighters (including dog). Note the sign arching over the doorway: "Public Library and Reading Room."

The library moved into the second floor above the fire station in 1886. Here librarian Lillian Rogers is pictured in the reading room. Library records show that in November of 1892, 651 males and 617 females visited the library, and there were 20 tickets for checkers.

In the early 1890's, Biddle Avenue was the scene of a major change when a street railway was installed. The street car was meant to be a more convenient way to reach Detroit and its neighbors than the earlier horse and buggy, boat or railroad. Service began on May 31, 1892. The fare was 15 cents to Detroit, one way, or 25 cents round trip. Street car service ended in 1932.

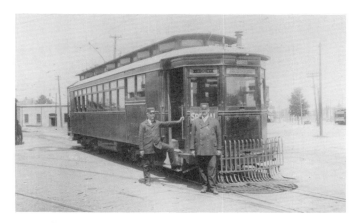

Some street cars were used for special duties. This is a funeral car.

The Detroit Suburban Street Railway was providing regularly scheduled streetcars down Biddle Avenue from Detroit to Trenton and beyond, every thirty minutes. Wyandotters complained that the drain on electrical power lines of the DSSR caused severe static on the few telephones that were in the city at that time.

Despite the street car tracks. Biddle was only cinders, mud and wagon ruts until 1905 when a contract for $41.076 was awarded for paving the Avenue with brick from Northline to Eureka. That same year the Detroit Railway agreed to install double tracks. In 1907, Biddle was paved from Eureka to Grove.

Pictured above is the west side of Biddle from Elm to Oak. A sale has attracted some customers. The Cahalan Brothers Drug Store on the near corner was built by William Belleville. He built many other Wyandotte buildings including the MacNichol home and the original St. Patrick rectory.

Biddle Avenue, looking north and looking south, was a thriving area in 1896. Power poles were already visible, and sidewalks had been laid in front of City Hall the year before.

Wyandotte's Detroit Exchange Hotel provided all of that era's modern conveniences to the weary traveler, including stabling.

With unpaved streets and horses, this picture of Biddle Avenue looks a bit like the Old West.

Norman Bowbeer's dental office was fronted by an up-to-date wooden sidewalk for his patients.

Crosswalk construction at Biddle and Oak was a boost to downtown development.

Today's Eureka does not resemble the Eureka Road of days gone by. The area of 11th Street was totally rural.

John Bittorf owned a large farm south of Eureka and west of 11th Street. He also owned Wyandotte's first butcher shop and served two terms as Mayor. The Bittorf homestead still stands on 20th Street.

Maple Hall, located on the northeast corner of Maple and Third Streets, was the site of many political speeches and celebrations. It also served as a temporary classroom before St. Joseph's School was built. Note the sign advertising the Wyandotte Brewing Company.

The immense wooden hall on Elm and Fourth Streets was once the social home of the German Arbeiter Society. The entire community enjoyed the dances, concerts, graduations and political events staged there. In 1944 the VFW purchased the facility and used it until 1955 when St. Joseph Church was built on the site.

The Arbeiter Hall Saloon offered the finest local brews available. Almost any occasion was reason enough to have a celebration, and soon the Arbeiter Society could get enough wagons to fill a parade route through Wyandotte and beyond. The hitching post and wooden sidewalks made the Saloon a favorite rest stop and watering hole for horse and gentry alike.

Baseball was played in Wyandotte at least as early as 1867. In that year, Wyandotte resident Michael Weatherwax wrote to his brother telling the results of a game between his Wyandotte Stars and the Taylor Monitors. At the end of five innings, Wyandotte led 85 to 15. He further wrote that there was plenty of time to play the full nine innings, but the team from Taylor decided to call it a day.

By 1898, Jerome H. Bishop, Jr., recently returned from Yale University, brought his experience with him and coached the newly formed Wyandotte High School football team.

The Wyandotte Herald of March 11, 1888 stated: *"...A match with the 'slabbies' for $9.00 a side is being arranged for next Sunday, and probably will come off on the grounds of the first ward unless officers interfere."*

On April 6, 1907, Wyandotte's indoor baseball team traveled to Ann Arbor to play a game with Owosso. Trainloads of fans accompanied each team. Both teams considered themselves state champions from the previous year. Early in the game, the umpire made a disputed call in favor of Owosso. An outraged Wyandotte fan hit the ump with a chair. The ensuing melee resulted in several Wyandotters being taken into custody. The game was never finished.

Champion Oarsmen of 1892

COLUMBUS BUSHA   ED. B. NELLIS

WM. R. OCOBOCK   DR. N. T. LANGLOIS

Rowing teams first formed in 1875 and began winning races almost immediately at many different sites from Toledo to Port Huron. Strong teams again appeared in the 1920's. Above are some trophies and medals won by the championship boating crew of 1892.

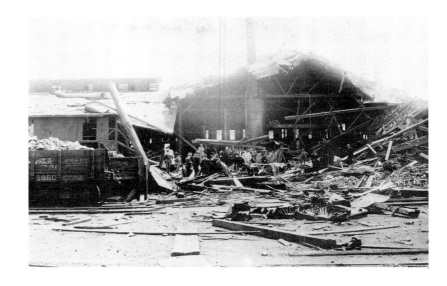

As the 1880's approached, Wyandotte's Eureka Iron Works and Rolling Mill was falling on hard times. Pig Iron prices had fallen below production costs. Charcoal was being railed in from over 200 miles away. A cheaper fuel was sought to smelt the iron ore. Core drillings found only salt beds, not the hoped for coal, gas or oil fields. An explosion at the Iron Works in 1888 rang the death knell for the industry in Wyandotte. After a fire in the remaining buildings in 1892, the rest of the works were dismantled. Soon afterward, Front Street was extended through the property from Elm to Eureka and renamed Van Alstyne Boulevard.

Captain John Baptiste Ford
1811-1905

While passing through Wyandotte on a railway car, Captain J. B. Ford heard that salt-beds were located under the city. He immediately got off the car and headed for the city hall. Known as "The Father of the Plate-Glass Industry," Captain Ford needed the source of salt to make Soda Ash, a principal ingredient of glass production. In 1890, he founded The Michigan Alkali Company along the south end waterfront and turned the city into a chemical town.

The Michigan Alkali Company's first plant was located along the river's edge in the south end of the city. Drilling rigs and wells marked the entire waterfront. The new industry brought a rebirth of prosperity and growth which affected every phase of city life, but the population would have to learn to tolerate the dust and the smells of the expanding chemical company.

In 1895, a second plant was built north of Northline Road along the river. Workers were needed and a large influx of Italian laborers and their families became part of the growing chemical industry in the area. The basic products of soda ash ("sodee ash"), baking soda and caustic soda were used to produce soaps, cleansers, cooking products and purifying agents. A third plant, The J. B. Ford Company, followed in 1898, and soon their products were selling throughout the world.

The Bishop home was immense when built in 1887. It had twenty large rooms, ten fireplaces, and an elegant third floor ballroom. The Bishop home was the social center for Wyandotte businessmen, church leaders and city government officials.

Jerome Holland Bishop's residence stood on Biddle Avenue at Superior Boulevard. In 1935, the family made the beautiful home available to Wyandotte for use as a City Hall. It was at that time that extensive renovations involved removing the massive porch circling the building.

Mr. Bishop's involvement in the community included supporting numerous churches and founding the Wyandotte Boat Club.

The Bishop home library held his extensive book collection. His interests in literature led him to provide funds matching city and school budgets to create a public library.

The ballroom was lavishly decorated and must have been an exciting setting for many social events hosted by the Bishops. The huge mirror on the left wall now is on display in the MacNichol Home Museum.
When the home was remodeled into a City Hall, the furnishings were sold off to the public. Today, many Wyandotters boast of a "Bishop Home" artifact.

Katherine Rattray, a Wyandotte resident, sketched a series of historically significant buildings.

John Stewart, a Protestant Methodist missionary arrived in the Indian village in 1816. The first religious gathering in Wyandotte was held by the Methodists in 1855. A cornerstone for this round church at Oak and Biddle was laid on June 12, 1899. The building was razed in 1964, and a new church, The First United Methodist Church, was erected on the same site.

Polish residents worshipped at St. Patrick and St. Joseph Churches before organizing Our Lady of Mt. Carmel Church in 1899. Dedication of a building on Tenth Street at Superior Blvd. was held on July 8, 1900. The present church, built in 1915, is of Italian Renaissance style.

From 1892, the Congregationalists worshipped with the Episcopalians in the Old Brown School. The cornerstone for the present church was laid in 1902. A gift of Jerome Holland Bishop, the building is Old English Gothic style, made of stone and paving brick, and patterned after Shakespeare's church at Stratford on Avon.

St. Charles Roman Catholic Church was built in 1857 on Superior at First. The two-story frame building, the Village of Wyandotte's first formal church building, was moved west in the same block in 1873 to provide for a larger brick church. During construction, a strong wind razed one of the walls, and construction was not resumed until 1883. The Church became known as St. Patrick's Roman Catholic Church about 1888.

Charles Warmbier, Jr. donated the Fifth and Sycamore corner lot for the Immanuel Lutheran Church and parsonage. Members assisted with labor and finances to ready the church for dedication in 1894. The building's architecture is of New England style with plain square lines. The church became a member of the American Synod.

In 1870, German members of St. Patrick's established St. Joseph's Church (not pictured) to enable the use of the German language in its services. It was located near the site of the present church and was built in 1871 at Elm and Fourth.

This sketch appeared in the Wyandotte Herald of December 31, 1897. The newspaper boasted that Mr. Edward Ford's new residence on the corner of Biddle and Vine was "an ornament" to Wyandotte. In 1942, the family moved to California and donated the house for use as a public library.

This photo of the house in the 1960's from nearly the same angle shows the Queen Anne style. It features a tower, a carriage port, a wide mosaic porch, 27 rooms and 11 fireplaces.

This is a later sketch of the Ford-Bacon Home. Since 1943, the structure has served as the Bacon Memorial Library.

80

Mark and Mary Ford Bacon made the Ford-Bacon Home their family home from 1902-1942. Mary was the daughter of Edward Ford and grand-daughter of J. B. Ford, founder of the Michigan Alkali Company. Mark was a lawyer and, in 1917, a member of the U. S. House of Representatives. He was one of the few to vote against U. S. entry into World War I.

The following photos of the interior of the Ford-Bacon Home from about 1905 reveal elegant rooms of oak panels, leaded glass and bay windows.

The main hallway looking toward Biddle

The reception room features a ceiling to floor fireplace and mantle. This was a favorite sitting room of the family.

More interiors of the Ford-Bacon House

Another view of the same room shows the main staircase which leads to a stained glass window on the landing.

The parlor on Biddle was decorated in green and gold with brocaded satin walls. This room was used to entertain guests but otherwise not used by the family.

The dining room featured a built-in-buffet, leaded glass cabinet, bottled windows and murals on the ceiling. A butler's pantry connects this room with the kitchen.

The billiards room featured oak paneling and window seats along two sides. There are niches on the east wall for the cues. This room served as a place to relax after dinner.

The walls of the library were of silk velour. Built-in bookcases with leaded glass doors run along one wall, and opposite them is an ornately carved fireplace mantle.

This aerial view shows three Biddle Avenue mansions between Vinewood and Superior Blvd. From left to right are the Bacon, Hurst and Bishop homes.

The 14 room Hurst home, constructed in 1880, was the residence of Mr. & Mrs. James Hurst and their two daughters and son. James Hurst settled in Wyandotte in 1867, established a lumbering business in 1869, and had a partnership in a lumber mill on Lake Superior. The three Hurst children never married and lived in the house until their deaths. The home was willed to the Board of Education by the late John Bacon. The prohibitive cost of correcting code violations resulted in the decision to raze the building in 1965.

Styles of advertising change, like everything else.
The *Wyandotte Herald* of September 6, 1895 ran these bits of verse.

JOHN BIGLER.

Meat Market.

Fresh steak, chops and cutlets,
Nice roasts of beef and veal
Are at John Bigler's market
To serve each daily meal.
Kept at his market in ice vaults clean and
  new—
Everything ice cold and sweet in readiness
  for you.
He has on hand the choicest
Of mutton, pork and lamb,
Nice corned beef and sausage
As well as sugar-cured ham.
His hands are well experienced,
And will cut for you a roast
So neatly, quick and easy
He has reason much to boast.
So remember well our counsel
Before this leaves your sight—
John Bigler runs the market
Where your meats are right.

FRED GINZEL.

General Store.

Fred Ginzel is prepared at any hour
To supply the demand for groceries and flour
Sugar, coffee, spices, cheese,
The very best in the line of teas.
He is a pusher and has a fine trade
Which he's earned selling goods of highest grade.
Crockery, tinware, china and glass—
Examine his stock as by you pass.
Boots and shoes for the young and old,
Dry goods and notions are at Ginzel's store sold.
Everything kept in a general stock
With prices always down to bed rock.
Buy the best in the market;
Sell as cheap as you can;
Leaving a profit to live on,
Is Fred Ginzel's plan.
Try him just once if you have not before;
Square dealing awaits you at his store.

WYANDOTTE CITY MILL.

T. C. Gray, Prop.

Bad flour makes bad bread,
Bad bread makes one wish he were dead,
Indigestion, dyspepsia, our deadly foes,
Cause many men to turn up their toes.
Wyandotte City Mill flour buy,
Made from good wheat for you and I,
Then you in truth can say,
"Physic to the dogs! I'll not pay
Money good for doctors' bills.
I've no aches. I've no ills."
Gold medal flour is made at home.
And makes good muscle, flesh and bone,
So let us pound you on the back,
Not very hard—an easy whack,
While in your ear we gently holler,
"Encourage home industry—buy Gold
  Medal Flour."

J. S. JOHNSON.

Horseshoeing and Blacksmithing.

Bad shoeing cripples horses—
Crippled horses cause a loss—
It pays to have them well shod
No matter what the cost.
J. S. Johnson, the blacksmith,
Is an artist in his line—
His horseshoeing and repairing,
Gives satisfaction every time.
As we listened to the music
Of his anvil's merry ring
With praise of his workmanship
Its echoes seemed to sing.
So remember well our council
Before this leaves your sight:
Johnson is the horseshoer
Who will shoe your horses right.

Wyandotte, being located between Detroit and Toledo, was in a position to see the best amusements. Companies appearing in leading playhouses were willing to book an extra run in Wyandotte.

The Marx Opera House opened October 8, 1896 on the west side of Biddle Avenue between Maple and Sycamore Streets. It was destroyed by a fire in June of 1908, but rebuilt in 1910 at Biddle and Sycamore.

Social gatherings were held in the Opera House because the first floor was level and could be used for dancing. We can see from a posted notice, the owners attempted to maintain a semblance of decorum:

> No intoxicated persons will be admitted
> No pushing or crowding
> No loud talking
> No profane or obscene language
> No whistling or other noise that would annoy the audience
> No throwing of missles (sic)
> No smoking
> No spitting on the floor
> No stomping of feet
> No defacing of seats or any part of the house

In the 1890's, the city's population rose to 5000. The bare bones factory town was now gaining some refinement with an increase in school and church activities and the rise of social clubs. The decade saw the formation of the Wyandotte Drama Club, the Tuesday Study Club and the first hospital. Circuses were popular and the bicycle craze ran its course.

Alex and Ephram Gohl pose in their Glenwood Tigers uniforms. Beginning in 1902, the area from the railroad tracks to 14th Street was the Village of Glenwood. Wyandotte annexed the area in 1905.

The Fourth of July was celebrated with parades and picnics. Here a band performs on July 4, 1890. Ari Woodruff is at far right.

In 1896, Edward Ford built a mansion at 2610 Biddle Avenue, the former site of Major John Biddle's home, and presented it to his daughter Laura and her husband George P. MacNichol, M. D. as a wedding gift. The Queen Anne style home features a turret with conical roof, projecting gables, and a wrap-around porch with a bannister of 500 spindles.

George P. MacNichol, baby Edward Ford MacNichol, Carrie Ross Ford, Grandmother Ross and Laura Ford MacNichol.

The formal parlor displays an oval portrait of Major John Biddle, whose house once occupied the site.

The Ford-MacNichol home, now the site of the Wyandotte Museum, has been furnished to reflect a late Victorian style.

The informal parlor is now exhibited as a music room.

The grand staircase has a bannister of 79 spindles, and woodwork of lavish golden oak.

The dining room has tall French doors leading to the porch, and features a grand mirror originally hung in the Bishop home.

The third floor includes a servant's room and bath. Note the wooden rim on the bathtub.

The master bedroom on the second floor features a turret sitting area. There is an adjoining dressing room and bathroom.

The library fireplace has a hearth of 92 imported Blue Delft tiles, each depicting a different scene of Holland. The coal burning fireplace has an ornate bronze grate.

The entrance hall fireplace features a clock by Silas B. Terry, from about 1840.

The front parlor fireplace is made of oak with an onyx and marble hearth. A beveled oval mirror and coupled columns supporting the mantle add to the elegant appearance.

The dining room fireplace includes a hearth of small tile pieces, a rectangular mirror, oak woodwork and ornate grill.

The Drennan family was the second to occupy the home presently known as the Ford-MacNichol House, 2610 Biddle. The Drennans lived there over sixty years.

The Drennan sisters not only claimed seniority at the first annual Wyandotte high school graduates' reunion; they also were the "mostest" from one family to be present. They posed under the "Class of '97" umbrella because Bernadette Drennan (third from left) was the only representative of that first Wyandotte High class to attend the gathering.

Shown with Bernadette are her sisters, Josephine (Class of 1913), Katherine, and Marguerite Drennan Whitty (Class of 1910).

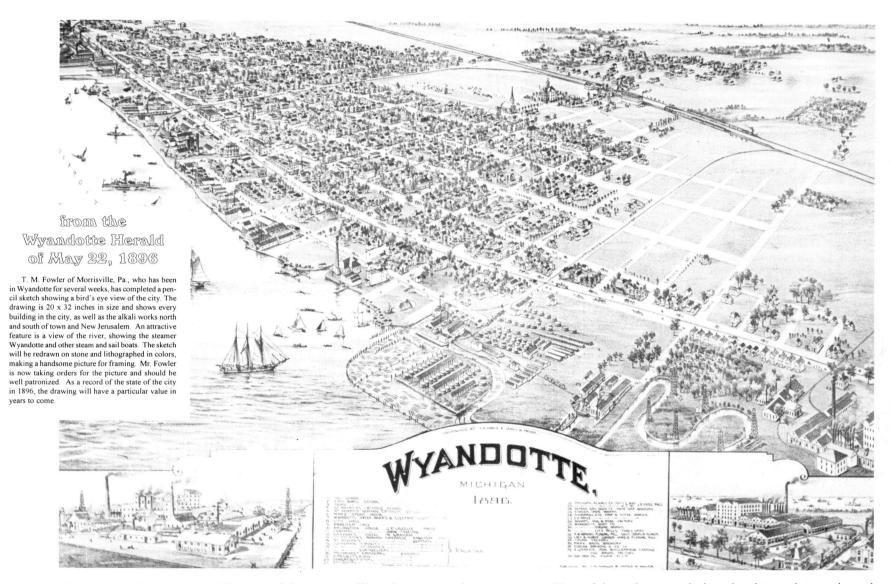

from the
Wyandotte Herald
of May 22, 1896

T. M. Fowler of Morrisville, Pa., who has been in Wyandotte for several weeks, has completed a pencil sketch showing a bird's eye view of the city. The drawing is 20 x 32 inches in size and shows every building in the city, as well as the alkali works north and south of town and New Jerusalem. An attractive feature is a view of the river, showing the steamer Wyandotte and other steam and sail boats. The sketch will be redrawn on stone and lithographed in colors, making a handsome picture for framing. Mr. Fowler is now taking orders for the picture and should be well patronized. As a record of the state of the city in 1896, the drawing will have a particular value in years to come.

WYANDOTTE,
MICHIGAN
1896.

As the young city approached the turn of the century, Wyandotte was truly a river town. Most of the industry, including the shipyard, was along the waterfront. The silent remains of the Eureka Iron Company still stood between Elm and Eureka Avenue, but the Michigan Alkali Company at both ends of the city would make Wyandotte a chemical town. Homes were reaching out toward Northline Road on the north, Grove Street on the south and the railroad tracks to the west. The settlement beyond the tracks was known as Glenwood. The section north of Northline would soon become the Village of Ford.

Wyandotte's city directory of 1898-99 listed a large number of businesses along Biddle Avenue, giving the city a well defined business district or "downtown."

Chestnut - Oak
BOWLES, E. A., 128 Biddle N., Photographer
THE FRANKLIN STORE, 116 Biddle N., "dime store"
SHOEMAKER DAIRY FARM, Leave orders at the Franklin Store
DR. NORMAN BOWBEER, Dental Office
MORGANTHAU, M. M., 102 Biddle N., Merchant Tailor
PRAY, SYLVESTER, 100½ Biddle N., Attorney at Law, Real Estate
PEARL, J. S. & HAMMOND, F. L., 100 Biddle N., Attorneys

Oak - Elm
ARLINGTON HOTEL, 99 Biddle N.
FIRST COMMERCIAL AND SAVINGS BANK, cor Oak and Biddle, E. Side
WISEMAN BROS., Under the Bank, Shave, Shampoo, Haircut, Baths
SMITH & NEGELSPACH'S, 98 Biddle N., Cut Flowers
HINDS, E. S., 96 Biddle N., Caterer, Ice Cream Parlor
REAUME, THOMAS, 96 Biddle N., Maker New Harness
STEELE, ALFRED, 93 Biddle N., Real Estate, Fire, Life, Accident Ins.
DELISLE, J. B., 93 Biddle N., Legal Papers
EBERTS, H. A., 93 Biddle N., Downtown Agency
McGLAUGHLIN, 93 Biddle N., Watches, Clocks, Jewelry
CONGREYER, A., Watchmaker in charge of Jewelry Dept.
BAUMLER HOUSE, G.A., Prop., 92-92½ Biddle N., Bar, Rest., Cafe
GENTHE & GIRARDIN, 89 Biddle N., Chase & Sanborn, Importers
THOMAS' DRUG STORE, 87 Biddle N.
CLARK, EVERETTE N., Son of Isaac Clark, Hardware
POST OFFICE, 86 Biddle N.
DETROIT EXCHANGE HOTEL, E. Side of Biddle
MILSPAUGH, Stable, E. Side of Biddle
DORRANCE & GARRISON, 80 Biddle N., Drugs, Stationery, Books
WAYMAN COAL CO., Office, 81 Biddle N.
CAHALAN, RICHARD & JOHN C., 79 Biddle N., In 1899, Telephone
    Exchange located over the Drug Store.
BLOODGOOD AND CO., 82 - 82½ Biddle N., Peninsula Stoves and Ranges
DOYLES BLDG., NE cor Biddle and Elm

Elm - Maple
WYANDOTTE SAVINGS BANK, SE cor Biddle and Elm, Est. 1871
CITY HALL, SW cor Biddle and Elm, built 1880

ROEHRIG, HENRY, & McINERNEY, JOHN F., Over Wyandotte Savings
    Bank, Leading Insurance Agents, Office
MELODY, JAMES B., JOHN T., GEORGE O., sons of John Melody, who
    came in 1855 from Ireland to work in the Eureka Iron Mill. 69 - 70 - 71
    Biddle N., Clothing and fine Household Store, est. 1895. First to apply
    for incandescent lamps from City.
MASONIC HALL, 76 Biddle N.
FURY, E. D., 65 Biddle N., Barber
FURY, WM., 63 Biddle N., Footwear and Repair

Maple - Sycamore
GORMAN, WM. F., 45 Biddle N., Cafe, Restaurant, Poolroom
MARX OPERA HOUSE, 39 - 41 Biddle N.
SULLIVAN, MISS M., 37 Biddle N., Fine Millinery
WILLIAMS, MRS. JULIA, 37½ Biddle N., Flour Mill, Feed and Grain
MACE & ATCHINSON, 41 Biddle N., General Hardware, Stoves and Ranges
    (Under the Opera House)

Sycamore - Eureka
H. C. THON, HENRY AND CHRIS, 23 - 25 Biddle N., Embalmers
KAUL, JOHN, HENRY AND WILLIAM, 19 - 21 Biddle N., Department Store,
    est. 1880, Had first stone sidewalk in front of store.
GARTNER, JOSEPH AND CHARLES, 17 Biddle N., est. 1882
LOEFFLER, AUGUST, 13 - 15 Biddle N., Department Store
ROEHRIG, MISS K., over Loeffler's 2nd floor
CRESCENT HOTEL, 2 Biddle N., Thos. Drouillard, Prop.

Eureka South
NIAGARA LAUNDRY, 14 - 16 Biddle S., Oscar Stieler, Prop., bought White
    Swan Steam Laundry from E. H. Fortenbaugh, 1898, (foot of Oak Street)
ATCHISON'S, P. E., Agency for Bicycles
FARNSWORTH, WM & CO., 18 Biddle S., Bicycles
KREGER, WM J., 22 Biddle S., In 1888 bought half a block of business
    frontage at Pine and Biddle, Boots, Shoes, Harness
KREGER, CHARLES, 58 - 60 Biddle S., Grocer
CORRIGAN HOTEL, 62 Biddle S.
COMMERCIAL HOTEL, cor Biddle and Orange, Louis Riopelle, Prop.
GRAHAM HOTEL, 138 - 140 Biddle S., Michael, G., Sr., Prop.

The Business District in 1896

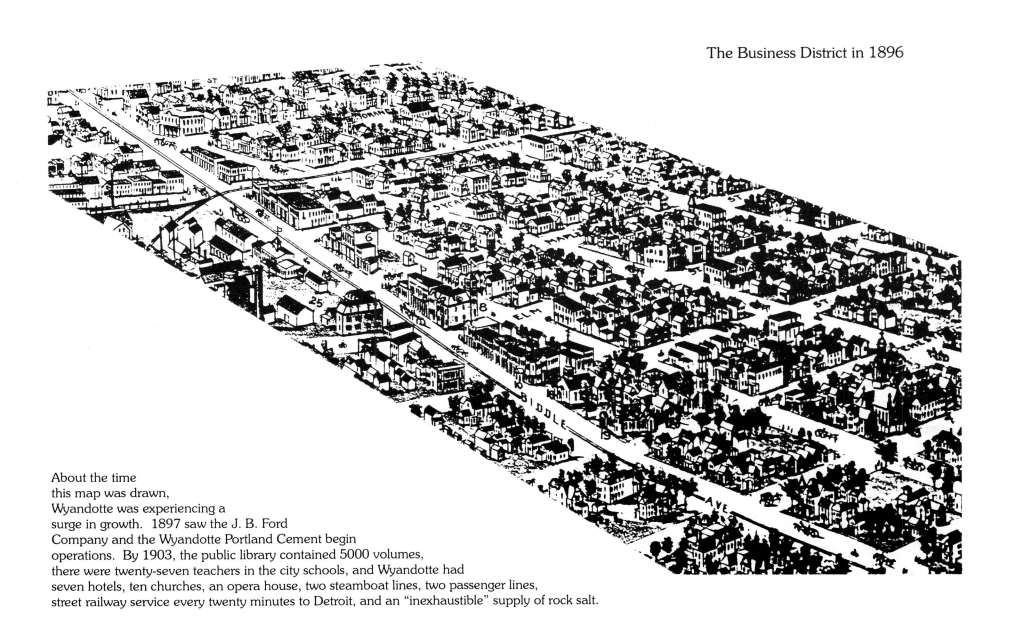

About the time
this map was drawn,
Wyandotte was experiencing a
surge in growth. 1897 saw the J. B. Ford
Company and the Wyandotte Portland Cement begin
operations. By 1903, the public library contained 5000 volumes,
there were twenty-seven teachers in the city schools, and Wyandotte had
seven hotels, ten churches, an opera house, two steamboat lines, two passenger lines,
street railway service every twenty minutes to Detroit, and an "inexhaustible" supply of rock salt.

1898 saw our country involved in the Spanish American War. Back home, Wyandotte seemed to be thriving. In what today may have seemed ahead of its time, female entrepreneurs were proudly advertising their local businesses.

Did you know that, according to the 1898/9 Wyandotte City Directory, Morton Salt Company, which had been incorporated a year earlier, maintained an office on Biddle Avenue S.?

When five-year-old Ralph J. Nixon was attracted to the black horses behind C. E. Neuendorf, Funeral Director and Furniture, no one could have imagined that he would also become drawn to the business. By 1909, the firm's name became Neuendorf and Nixon. In 1923, Ralph Nixon purchased the Neuendorf interest and began Nixon, Undertaker and Furniture Dealer. In 1927, he located at Biddle and Vinewood, devoting his efforts to the undertaking service.

The Eureka Brewing Company was founded in 1890 at Van Alstyne and Poplar and gave some competition to the Marx Brewery established 27 years earlier. The two breweries consolidated in 1910.

In 1906, tired of waiting for zero degree weather to freeze the river, the brewery built its own ice plant for $10,000.

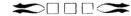

In the 1870's, newly-weds John and Emma Eberts boasted of having the first coal stove in Wyandotte. But there was no coal dealer in town, cord wood being the common source of home fuel. Mr. Eberts bought a carload of coal, which eventually led to his involvement in the coal business.

In 1890, he established a coal company on Front Street (Van Alstyne) near Walnut Street. By the turn of the century, the Eberts Brothers Company was run by his sons Harry, Frank and Walter.

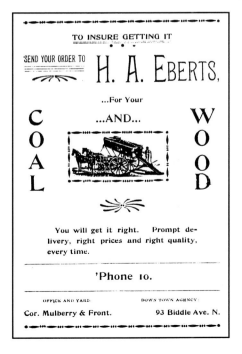

This receipt from Labadie Brothers, a rival coal dealer, reads: "2 ton KY Lump $18.00." Note the house address: "Second house past car line on Goddard."

101

Wyandotte, High School, Wyandotte, Mich.

The Lincoln High School was a beautiful brick building with separate entrances for boys and girls. Construction costs of $52,000 were a major investment in 1905. With the opening of the Roosevelt High School in 1923, the school was renamed Lincoln Junior High School. Intermediate grades were housed in the building until 1956, when a new Abraham Lincoln Junior High was built in southwest Wyandotte. The Wyandotte Board of Education Administration Building later occupied the site.

Hazel Adair and her first grade class pose in their finest dress in 1915 outside the old Garfield School.

Hazel Adair went on to work at the Carnegie Library and eventually became Director of the Bacon Memorial Library at Biddle and Vinewood.

In 1886, the First Ward School was built at Third and Superior. The building pictured here replaced the original in 1898, and was renamed Garfield School in 1905. In 1932, a new, larger Garfield School was built on the site.

John Classon stands on the steps of his grocery store on Fourth Street between Chestnut and Superior. The small structure under the tree was used to dispense kerosene.

The gang at Ed Asmus' Sample Room at Orange and Sixth Streets step outside for a group photo. Ed is third from the left. His brother Emil is at the center with apron. All are sampling, except of course the children, one of whom prefers a good cigar.

This gathering in front of the Adolph Shultz Saloon shows the clothing styles for men, women and children.

This is the former Roehrig home on Biddle Avenue which was later occupied by the Wabeek Tea Room.

Conrad and Henry Roehrig operated the Roehrig Brothers Store from 1910 to 1939. In 1940, the building became the largest of three Cahalan stores in the city.

ROEHRIG BROTHERS.
CLOTHING, HATS, AND GENTLEMEN'S FURNISHINGS.
Wyandotte, Mich.

I am a REAL ESTATE AGENT, you see.
Some day you'll be wanting a place of me.
So to all I implore,
Come and see me at my store,
For I sell lands of every kind—
The cheapest and best that you'll ever find.
Then be sure to give me a call,
Whether ye be stout, lean, lank or tall.

HENRY ROEHRIG.

John J. Kreger and his descendants operated businesses in Wyandotte for nearly 100 years. Much of this activity took place at the southeast corner of Fifth and Eureka.

JOHN   J.   KREGER,

—Headquarters for—

Farming Implements, Buggies,

Carriages, Wagons, Etc.
Farm and Garden Seeds
that are sure to grow.

Wood   Yard

Constantly stocked with hard and soft wood. If you are in need of anything in my line I can save you money and give you the best in the market.

. . . **Repairs of all kinds.**

Implement Dealer.   -   Auctioneer.

Cor. Eureka and Fifth.

All kinds farm implements always on hand. The best for the lowest price.

An ad from 1898.

John Kreger stands proudly with his five children in front of his farm implement store and home.

About 1894, the Kregers began bottling soda pop at the farm implement shop.

The interior of the bottling plant, about 1905.

John J. Kreger, John P. Kreger and Conrad P. Kreger are pictured standing at Eureka and Fifth at their new Star Bottling Company building in 1913. The building was the first reinforced concrete structure in the city. The Kreger's first truck was a chain-driven Horner. Horner Trucks were built at Fourth and Mulberry Streets. In 1923, Kreger Beverages Company acquired the Coca-Cola franchise. By the 1930's, the business became known as the Wyandotte Coca-Cola Bottling Company, Inc. The building at the rear of the bottling works still housed the horses and farm implement business.

The Gartner family business started with groceries in the 1870's and a hardware store by 1882.

The family was very civic minded. Joseph was president of the first fire department in 1886, and William became the first native born mayor of the city in 1898.

By 1900, the family business included gas service. In that year, they donated land for the building of Our Lady of Mount Carmel Church.

Just as many local businesses do today, Gartner's sponsored a local baseball team.

The Mehlhose family ice cream business extends over a hundred years through Wyandotte history. John Davis and Milton Howe are pictured at the turn-of-the-century with a horse drawn delivery wagon. Note the milk cans. Milk bottles would not be used until about 1910. In deep snow, the wagon would be replaced by a bobsled.

Entering a float in the German Day Parade was good for business.

An ad from the 1899 Wyandotte High School Year Book reveals that ice cream was a special treat, delivered especially for Sunday dinner.

Oak Street was a busy commercial area around the turn of the century. In 1909, Charles Bigler opened a new meat shop at Oak and Second. By then, the family had over 30 years of business experience in Wyandotte.

An ad in the 1899 high school year book was a good place for the bakery to advertise since it was within easy walking distance of the school, then also on Oak.

An early merchant on the northwest corner of Oak and First Streets was the Nelson Dupy Grocery Store. In later years, the wooden store was replaced with a block building that would become the Niagara Laundry.

The First Commercial and Savings Bank Building was built in 1893 on the southeast corner of Oak and Biddle, and still stands today. Many of the city's doctors and dentists had offices there, including Dr. William Honor and Dr. Norman Bowbeer.

Some of the people at the Northline Cafe pose for this photo about 1900. Something about the cafe looks like it could exist a century later.

August Hoffman and his son Louis are pictured in front of the family shoe store on Orange Street near Fifth. The rolled bundles of hides are evidence that shoes were made on the premises. In 1880, a pair of shoes cost two dollars and took two days to make. Note the boot sign also.

The Hoersch Shoe store was offering a real bargain, shoes for 98¢, cheap even in those days.

At the turn of the century, these stately homes graced Biddle Avenue in the Poplar and Vinewood area. Residents included the Eberts, Nellis and Fairchild families.

The 1905 christening of a new baby boy was cause for celebration in the Czarnecki household on Sixth Street. The baby was given the name Harry. As an adult, his musical talent would earn him the name Trumpet Harry.

This 1906 photo shows Beatrice Bowbeer, Carrie Fairchild and Norma Bowbeer sitting outside the Bowbeer home on Biddle.

By the first decade of the Twentieth Century, Biddle Avenue was well established with sidewalks, curbs and electricity. In 1906, it was paved with brick block on a concrete foundation from Northline to Eureka at the cost of $41,000, creating a thoroughfare 20 feet wider than Detroit's Woodward Avenue.

The George Payne, Jr. home (2533 Biddle) was built in 1902. The house was arranged with an open space reaching to the roof so Mr. Payne could work on his hobby of perpetual motion, trying to overcome the effects of gravitation and friction.

1903 saw the establishment of the City's first uniformed police force...the Chief and three patrolmen. In 1907, it was noted that Wyandotte had 51 saloons and two breweries. By 1908, a full time fire department was needed. By 1909, the population had reached 9,000.

Following the demolition of the abandoned Eureka Iron Works and Rolling Mill, Front Street was extended from Oak to Eureka and renamed Van Alstyne Boulevard. Soon a row of fashionable homes filled the newly platted riverfront.

Robert Burrell "drives" his passengers Howard Clark and Lila Fairchild.

The Rafter Family

Neighborhood sidewalks became common in the early 1900's. Families gathered on their porches to socialize, and children played the games of yesteryear. Here, baby Beatrice Bowbeer tries out the new sidewalk.

Young Alex Freytag, standing next to his father in their back yard, began working at Bishop Fur Company when he was fourteen years old. Later, as an adult, he would operate Freytag Furs on Biddle Avenue.

The Max Freytag family gathers in front of their home at the corner of Fourth and Vine in 1903. Mr. Freytag was a superintendent at Bishop Fur Company. A large stable may be seen behind the house.

The Parish Family gathers for a reunion picture.

The Loranger Hotel, built in 1901, stood at Third and Plum Streets. Many shipyard employees enjoyed the comfort and convenience of this nearby hotel.

Wyandotte Hotel, 1914, Corner of First and Elm Streets

The growing industries in Wyandotte attracted many laborers. Company Houses and numerous hotels provided housing for workers until they could purchase their own homes.
Some hotels in Wyandotte:

1856	Biddle House, Major John Biddle's house used as a stagecoach stop
1865	Railroad House, Oak and First Streets, proprietors, Joseph and Margaret Roehrig
1867	Johnson House, between Oak and Elm
1875	Quinn Hotel, Biddle and Orange
	1888 - 98 Commercial Hotel, same location
	1907 - 08 Alvoy Hotel, same location
1881	Campbell House
1888	Baumler House, 92 Biddle, proprietor, G.A. Baumler
1907	Union Hotel, 46 Elm, built by Frank Marx
1907	Ewald Hotel, 264 Oak
1915	Central House, 236 Oak
1915	Mollno Hotel, 399 Biddle, Ford City
1915	Tashmoo Hotel, Pine and Third
1915	Riverview House, Biddle and Central, proprietor, Fred C. Miller

Marx Hotel, 1905, Corner of Biddle and Alkali, Ford Village

The Willamma was built in 1900 by Will and Amma Denman at the southeast corner of Biddle and Chestnut. It boasted hot and cold water on every floor and dining for one hundred. Waitresses wore black uniforms at breakfast and white for dinner. It was renamed the Columbia in 1901, and the Parkview in 1923.

From 1915 to 1941, the Carnegie Public Library stood on the east side of Biddle, between Maple and Sycamore Streets. It was the first building constructed solely for use as a library. The building was built without cost to the taxpayers through a grant from industrialist Andrew Carnegie. There was some opposition to accepting the grant, since Carnegie's attitude toward the laboring class did not sit well with many blue collar Wyandotters.

A look inside the library in 1941 shows head librarian Hazel Adair at the charging desk.

Another view of the library shows librarian June Schroeder.

Trinity Lutheran School at Oak and Fifth Streets was one of several parochial schools in Wyandotte that added "Religion" to the other 3 R's of education. This photo dates from about 1910.

In 1900, Captain John B. Ford gave $500 toward the building of a clubhouse for the employees of the Michigan Alkali and J. B. Ford Companies. The land area, now Bishop Park, was used as a dumping ground for Eureka Iron Company cinders, and was known as "Cinder Park." The American Legion would later occupy the building. The two photos on the right show the building from the river side and the street side.

In 1905, the Frank Marx Dancing Pavilion opened at the foot of Oak Street. The first floor contained a boat house and sitting rooms. Three wide stairways, beautifully lit by electricity, led to a large dance floor on the upper level.

A sailboat owned by Louis Shomberg floats in front of a summer cottage and boat house built by Albert and Joseph Daniel, at the foot of Orange Street, sometime after 1910.

As these photos show, when industry relinquished its use of Burrell Slip, year round recreation became its successor. Many private boat houses and rowing facilities were built. The site was also popular for public swimming, ice skating and ice fishing.

Excursions on the river were a popular pastime. Boats such as the *Tashmoo*, *Wyandotte* and *Riverside* would embark for Sugar Island, Bois Blanc (Bob-Lo) and Put-In-Bay for a day of camping, picnicking, dancing, swimming, sports or amusement rides.

Captain John DeSana was born in Amherstberg, Ontario in 1840 and settled in Wyandotte during the 1860's. He served on the *Riverside* and the steamer *Wyandotte*. Later he purchased the steamer *Douglas* which he captained until 1908. He often gave children a free ride. A second boat, the *Fremont* was added to his operations for freight only.

The steamer *Wyandotte* was built in Wyandotte in 1892. She made her trial run in October, running from Detroit to Bois Blanc at the speed of 17.5 mph against a stiff southwest wind. The *Wyandotte* carried freight and up to one thousand passengers daily. It sailed to Detroit at 7:45 am and returned at 4:00 pm. The round trip fare was 8.5 cents when purchased in lots.

Wyandotte's Big Day
Board of Commerce Annual Excursion
SUGAR ISLAND
Thursday, June, 14, 1923
Bigger and Better Than Ever!!

The Tashmoo and Greyhound, finest steamers of the White Star Fleet, will carry the crowd.

Free Dancing on the boats and at the Island

A splendid program of High School track events.   Free for all events.

A base ball game between St. Patrick's and another team in their own league. This is a scheduled league game and will be a hot one.

A dandy bathing beach.   A Roller Coaster, Merry-Go-Round and other attractions for the Children. The best Cafeteria to be found in any park or resort around Detroit.

A long list of prizes, including lady's silk fiber sweater, a length of best quality silk dress goods, an exquisite luncheon cloth, case of Heinz products, men's caps, men's shirts, collars, belts and buckles, boxes of cigars, boxes of candy, a dandy coaster wagon for some lucky kid, a Spalding base ball glove, tennis shoes, loving cup and many other articles. Every prize is of first class quality.

There will be novelty stunts both on the boats and at the island.

Every kiddie will be given a souvenir.

IT'S YOUR DAY—COME YOURSELF AND BRING YOUR FAMILY

Boost This Big Day to Everyone You Meet—Thursday, June 14, at Sugar Island

Steamer *Put-In-Bay* launched March of 1911.

From the Wyandotte Herald of March 1911:
Master William McFall Heyser of Cincinnati, a grand-son of William McFall, has been selected by Ashley & Dustin to christen the latter's new passenger steamer, which will be launched at the Wyandotte shipyard on Saturday, March 18.

When it came time to name the new steamer, Ashley & Dustin Steamer Line ran a contest to name her. Over 2000 entries were submitted, with T. C. Gray of Wyandotte declared the winner. For his *Put-In-Bay* suggestion, he received a season pass and ten dollars.

The *Put-In-Bay* was the largest passenger ship built at the Wyandotte Shipyards. George Finsel's Orchestra was on the maiden voyage of the *Put-In-Bay* and he attended the final cruise before her official burning on October 3, 1953. Leader Finsel never missed a sailing.

The sidewheeler passenger steamer *Tashmoo*, in its day the fastest steamship on the Lakes, was launched at the Wyandotte Shipyards December 30, 1899. She was 320 feet overall, and represented an outlay of $250,000. She was capable of carrying 4000 people. President Theodore Roosevelt enjoyed a trip on the boat while visiting Detroit.

The *Shaughnessy* was launched May 25, 1906. Named after the President of the Canadian Pacific Railway, visitors were on hand from Toronto, Montreal, Cleveland, Pittsburgh and Detroit to witness her slide into the waters. The ship was then towed to Detroit to have her fitting-out completed.

In 1908, the freighter Wyandotte was the flagship of the J. B. Ford fleet. She was the world's first self-unloader, developed by engineer Robert Smith. She could carry 4330 tons of stone or 2800 tons of coal.

The Beals and Selkirk Trunk Company moved to Wyandotte in 1891. From its factory along the railroad tracks between Chestnut and Vine, it manufactured trunks of all shapes and sizes. After a fire in 1902, it was rebuilt. This sketch from 1916 shows a large and thriving industry.

Trunks in various stages of construction can be seen in this interior view. Beals and Selkirk trunks were sold throughout the United States, Canada and foreign countries. The factory closed in 1955.

Events of the world-at-large would occasionally reach into the small towns of America. When America went to war with Spain in 1898, 43 men of Wyandotte organized into a volunteer company. Late in the afternoon of June 30, 1898, a large crowd assembled at the railway station to see the boys off to war. A band played patriotic tunes followed by a short address by J. H. Bishop.

In February, 1899, the War Department issued the mustering out orders for the Wyandotte boys in Company F, Thirty-Fifth Michigan Volunteers. No crowd greeted the boys upon their return on April 2, 1899 owing to a report that the train bearing the soldiers would not stop here but go on through to Detroit.

On September 21, 1902, a crowd gathered at Union Station at Oak Street hoping to catch a glimpse of President Theodore Roosevelt on his way to Detroit. Shortly after this photo was snapped, the Presidential train comprised of six splendid coaches pulled into the station. The train slowed and President Roosevelt appeared on the rear platform of the last coach. With his left hand thrust in his trouser pocket, he waved a white handkerchief with his right, bowing and smiling in response to the crowd's enthusiastic greeting. The train then went on to Detroit.

Horse racing was popular locally from 1889 through the end of World War I. Within the city, the site of race activity was called "Forty Acres" and was located between Oak and Eureka on the present site of Roosevelt High School.

The half mile track at its peak of popularity included a sheltered grandstand. The old Lincoln School may be seen in the background.

BANNER RACES
of the Season Given by
THE WYANDOTTE DRIVING CLUB
AT
SINGER'S TRACK
ON
SEPT. 7, LABOR DAY, 1914

5 Minutes Walk from Toledo Line.   12 Miles from Detroit

$325.00 IN PURSES

2:29 Trot or Pace, Purse - - - $100.00   Free-for-All Trot or Pace, Purse - - $100.00
2:19 Trot or Pace, Purse - - - 100.00   Special Colt Race for local horses only 25.00

CONDITIONS OF RACES:

Cars will leave at every half hour, at Oak and Eureka, for race track. Refreshments served on Grounds

Admission 25 Cents. | FRANK NELLIS, Secretary

The Wyandotte Driving Association was the force behind organized racing in Wyandotte in the 1890's. Later, as in this newspaper ad from 1914, it was the Wyandotte Driving Club.

While the boys at old Central High School at Oak and Seventh Streets were busy playing football, the girls took to the hardwood court playing "Roundball." In 1899, through the promotion of Mrs. John S. Van Alstyne, two basketball teams were organized for the girls at Central High. The first team was coached by Miss Jean Dawson (middle row, fifth from left). Team members included such pioneer family names as Loeffler, Van Alstyne, Drennan, Babcock, Groh and Henning.

The Jager-Asmus Hardware Store on First near Maple is shown about 1920. Otto Asmus is on the left, his brother Emil on the right, with his arm on the counter. The store offered not only paint, glass, roofing and tools, but toys and sporting goods as well. In 1923, the store moved to 2944 Biddle.

Biddle St., Wyandotte, Mich.

This view of Biddle Avenue looks south from Oak Street toward Elm. The first building on the left is the McInerney Building. Nixon Funeral Home and furniture store stands at the far corner at Elm. Across Elm is Wyandotte Savings Bank. On the right side, the first structure is the Arlington Hotel. The next store is a sweet shop, and toward the middle of the block is the Grant Mertins Grocery and Thomas Drug Store.

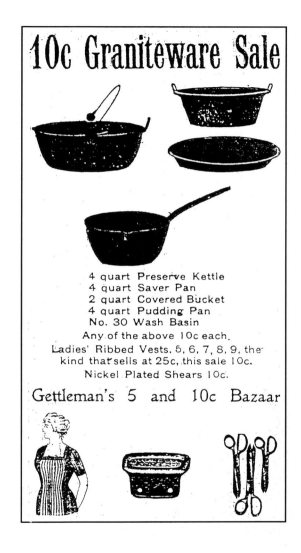

10c Graniteware Sale

4 quart Preserve Kettle
4 quart Saver Pan
2 quart Covered Bucket
4 quart Pudding Pan
No. 30 Wash Basin
Any of the above 10c each.
Ladies' Ribbed Vests, 5, 6, 7, 8, 9, the kind that sells at 25c, this sale 10c.
Nickel Plated Shears 10c.

Gettleman's 5 and 10c Bazaar

The two photos on this page show changes at the northwest corner of Biddle and Eureka. From about 1910, the businesses pictured from left to right are: Little Dry Goods, Gettleman's Bazaar, Genthe Groceries, H. Rosenthal clothing, unidentified, Gartner & Long Shoes, C. Loeffler Dry Goods and Gartner Hardware.

This photo, taken about 1915, shows Gettleman's Bazaar has relocated to the corner. Opened in 1902, it was an early example of the five and dime store. Note that the automobile has replaced the horse and buggy.

In 1904, Dwight Baxter built this automobile in a bicycle shop in the back of the Brohl Bakery on Eureka.

Mr. and Mrs. John Bittorf enjoy a ride on their Golden Wedding Anniversary in 1905. In the front are Mark Bacon and his chauffeur Fred Cory.

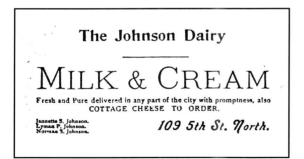

The Johnson Dairy

MILK & CREAM

Fresh and Pure delivered in any part of the city with promptness, also
COTTAGE CHEESE TO ORDER.

Jannette S. Johnson.
Lyman P. Johnson.
Norman S. Johnson.

109 5th St. North.

Johnson Creamery was established at Fifth and Chestnut Streets by Perry Johnson in 1886 and stayed in business for about 70 years.

There was a transition period of several years during which the horse and buggy and the automobile shared the streets. Here, in 1911, horse drawn delivery wagons line up outside Johnson Creamery ready to start their daily deliveries of fresh milk to home customers.

A. W. Pardo is credited with bringing the automobile to Wyandotte. In 1909, he sold his first Ford. In later years, he was franchised to sell Cadillacs, Hupmobiles, Overlands and Ford Motor Company products. In 1911, he built a garage and dealership on the east side of Biddle between Oak and Chestnut. For several years, Pardo's Garage was the only service garage between Detroit and Monroe. He also provided the first curbside gas pump and the first automobile taxi service in the city. The famous "Ford Racer" was built in Pardo's garage. In the above photo, Bill Pardo is the passenger in the racer with William Rummel at the wheel.

John D. "Jack" Brown worked in barber shops on Biddle Avenue for 35 years. At the right, he works with another barber, while below, he stands in the foreground in his own shop.

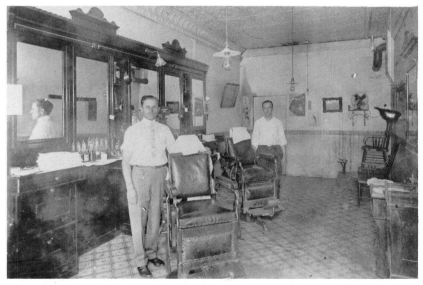

Barber chairs of leather or velour offered all the comforts of home. The barber shop was also a perfect place to exchange the news of the day. And what better place to get a shoe shine before heading on one's way.

Barbering in the good old days meant long, long hours that catered to the needs of faithful customers. Seldom was there time to leave for lunch or dinner and, sometimes hot meals were delivered from home.

"Regulars" left their personal shaving mugs and brushes at the barber shop, often to be stored in a wall rack. Mirror and cabinet units reflected the style of the day, including marble counter tops on which the many bottles of hair and face preparations were displayed.

136

There were other fire stations in Wyandotte before the central fire station was built at Maple and Third in 1939. The Ford Village Municipal Building was constructed in 1916 at a cost of $30,000. It housed the fire department, jail, council chambers and city offices. It was last used by the city of Wyandotte as a fire station. The historic edifice was razed in 1993.

The first floor of Wyandotte's old "City Hall", built in 1881, served as the main fire station until 1940. The site at the corner of Biddle and Elm was later occupied by Kinsel Drugs and the Willow Tree.

Beginning in 1914, the Detroit-Wyandotte Motor Truck Company, on Fourth Street from Mulberry to Cedar, manufactured the "Horner, The Truck Without A Fault." Officers were G. Horner, President and Manager; R. Parker, Secretary; John Marx, Treasurer. The plant produced 1 1/2, 2, 3 and 5 ton size trucks. Shipments were made as far away as Cuba and Puerto Rico.

A Hess "Bluebird" airplane is prepared for the Dole Race to Hawaii in 1927. Between 1926 and 1928, the Hess Airplane Company manufactured planes on the second floor of the former Marx Brewery garage on Van Alstyne Boulevard between Oak and Elm. The new airplane went on the market for $2250. Planes were tested and flown from an airfield at the Southwest corner of Fort Street and Eureka.

By the 1920's, the J. B. Ford Company developed hundreds of products that were distributed throughout the world. Thirty-three countries bought "Wyandotte Indian" logo soaps, detergents, cleansers, and food preparations. Initially the J. B. Ford Company had set out to "liberate the housewife from her slavery to cleaning." However, its products were widely used in businesses and industries as well as in homes.

The area from Northline Road to Ecorse Creek did not become part of the city of Wyandotte until 1922. Originally, it was Ecorse Township. In 1902, it became Ford Village, but was more often referred to as Ford City or Ford, Michigan.

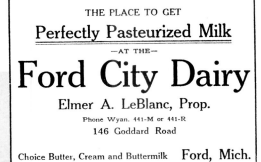

Helpers Lloyd Jarvis and Columbus LeBlanc stand with the Ford City Dairy wagon at 426 Goddard Road in 1922. Goddard was still a dirt-covered road that presented a challenge to horses and early autos in Ford City.

Ralph and Rosilda Meyer would soon be attending Wyandotte schools with the 1922 annexation of Ford City.

FORD

Ford, incorporated as a village in 1902, is located on the L S & M S, the M C and the D T & I R R's, immediately north of Wyandotte, and extends northerly along the Detroit River to Ecorse Village. The Detroit United Ry (Wyandotte Division), gives a 30-minute service to and from Detroit and all towns south to Trenton. The Detroit Monroe & Toledo Electric gives a sixty-minute service to Detroit and Toledo.

VILLAGE OFFICERS

President---Wm G Perry
Clerk---Milton R Mollno
Treasurer---Adolph Perry
Marshall---Geo. W. Perry
Deputy Marshal---Benjamin Donaldson
Assessor---Columbus San Souci
Health Officer---Dr H S Brodersen
Engineer---Mason L Brown
Fire Chief---Elmer A Labadie
Captain Fire Department---Oliver San Souci
Street Commissioner---Peter Labeau
Village Attorney---Ari E. Woodruff
Trustees---Chas. Begeman, Elmer LeBlanc, Ernest Labadie, Louis E. Goodell, Hiram McGlaughlin, John Foret.

FORD CITY SCHOOL BOARD

President, Selah Sanderson;   Secretary, Erastus LeBlanc
Superintendent, Chas. F. Pike   Treasurer, Antoine Labadie
Trustees: Wm. Berndt, Frank Labadie

Fred Torango's home was conveniently located next to his business on Biddle Avenue between Davis and Sullivan Streets. He operated Fred Torango Meats in 1915.

Flavo McLaughlin stands next to his car near the north-west corner of Oak and Biddle. This 1922 photo shows the dome of the First Methodist Church in the background.

Oh, the joys of early automobiling down Biddle Avenue between Orange and Eureka! Dwight Baxter navigates through the mud. Note the street car tracks along the way.

Katherine Laritz and her daughter, Frances, are in the family sweet shop about 1920. The shop was located in the basement of their home at Eureka near Thirteenth. In 1948, their son Frank with his wife, Victoria, built and operated the Ira Wilson & Sons dairy bar next door to the original Laritz Sweet Shop.

As the number of autos increased, road improvements soon followed. In 1928, viaducts were constructed over Eureka and the road was widened.

Wyandotte News Herald
August 14, 1931
The old horse drinking trough on Elm Street, between Biddle Avenue and First Street, was ordered removed and to be replaced by a drinking fountain for humankind.

Surveyors were at Eureka and Fifth Streets on October 10, 1921 to lay out the foundations for the new Theodore Roosevelt High School. Within days, men and teams of horses were busy constructing the school on the site that just a few years before was known as "Forty Acres Race Track." The new school was built to accommodate 1400 students and cost a staggering $1,140,000. Hundreds of Wyandotters found work on the project. Note the Brass Works along the tracks at the left, the Lincoln High School bell tower at far center, and the row of newly built homes along Sycamore Street.

When Theodore Roosevelt High School opened in 1923, the building was considered among the finest in the State. The earlier high school building became Lincoln Junior High School, and the elementary grades expanded and were housed in their own schools. Superintendent F. W. Frostic's dream of bringing the Wyandotte Public Schools into the 20th Century was realized with the building of Roosevelt High.

Continuing the Melody Brothers' long ventures into mercantile businesses in Wyandotte, Cecilia Melody opened her own Hosiery Shop in 1933 on Biddle Avenue. The stylish shop was very popular with the women of the area, and became even more so as she expanded her merchandise variety.

FEDERAL MEN STAGE SERIES OF LIQUOR RAIDS

Twenty federal enforcement officers ... H. Brennan, federal ... last

48 PERSONS TAKEN IN RAIDS WERE FINED

Following raids on roadhouses, cab... and saloons last Saturday night, ... arrested and told to ...

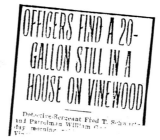

MUCH LIQUOR CONFISCATED IN SUNDAY RAIDS

In raids conducted last Sunday afternoon, by ten officers in charge of Deputy Commissioner of Public Safety Richard Elliott and Chief ... Sheriff Lester Dunn, 17 ... visited in a search ...

Among ... and

OFFICERS FIND A 20-GALLON STILL IN A HOUSE ON VINEWOOD

Detective-Sergeant Fred T. Schwartz and Patrolman William G... day morning ...

CHARGED WITH PLOT TO HELP SMUGGLING

... former chief

Police Seize a Truckload of Beer

The police, Tuesday night, captured a truck load of 85 cases of beer. It happened on Orange street, several blocks from Riddle. The driver ... truck, no doubt, went ... away with the ... that he ... th ...

WYANDOTTER CHARGED WITH RUM GRAFT

Approximately ... officers and ... been locked up by ... officers in the smuggling ... the Detroit river ...

RUMMERS GREW TIRED OF THEIR WINDSOR EXILE

Late in 1928, following a federal indictment of a lot of Detroit ... bition ...

During those exciting but tragic years of Prohibition (1918 - 1933), much of the downriver waterfront was a beehive of illegal activity in rum-running. Hauling liquor by boat from Canada to waiting trucks along darkened docks and coves was a thriving business. Gangland killings, mass arrests, and confiscations of illegal "booze" made the headlines then.

Beer, Auto and Boat Are Seized

Two automobile, a speed boat, and ... cases of beer were confiscated ... yesterday by two federal customs patrol guards on Grosse Ile ... last seizure took place near ... where two patrolmen ... boat and ...

ARRESTED AFTER GUN BATTLE

Two Boat-Loads of Beer Seized in River, Off Fighting Island

Three men were arrested and two boat-loads of beer were seized by agents of the Customs border patrol

BLIND PIGS FINED $800 IN FEBRUARY

The report of Chief of Police Clarence C. Chapman for the month of February shows that 14 persons ... arrested for vi...

The Knights of Columbus established in Wyandotte in 1915. In the twenties, they organized a drill team which won several competitions throughout the Midwest. This photo is from the 1925 Wyandotte Fourth of July Parade.

The Metropolitan Club engaged in charitable works, including bringing children to the Majestic Theatre at Christmas time. Note the marquis of the theatre in the late twenties advertising both the new talking movies with live entertainment.

The Sauer Cooperage on Goddard manufactured barrels for sugar and flour, kegs for nails, bolts and metals, and plywood drums used by creameries. It was one of many industries that lined the railroad corridor through Wyandotte, making it an industrial center. The plant was rebuilt after a fire in 1929.

In 1926, Wyandotte's two small hospitals were replaced with Wyandotte General Hospital, a gift of the J. B. Ford Family. When it opened, it had only 50 beds, but was quickly expanded. This aerial view was taken in 1933.

This view of Biddle Avenue looking north from Ford Avenue, about 1935, shows a flourishing business district in the former Village of Ford. The building housing the Hudson Terraplane Motor Company showroom still remains at the corner of Sullivan and Biddle.

Tommy Torango stands with his colt in front of the store and residence of G. H. Stoneburner on Biddle between Sullivan and Davis. This building is the third from the left in the larger photo above.

The building in the immediate foreground at Biddle and Clark served as home and barber shop for the Clifford Burke family. Mr. Burke would become a councilman for the City of Wyandotte in the 1940's.

Another view of Biddle Avenue in the former Ford Village, looking north from Antoine Street, shows the tall fence that bordered the Wyandotte Chemicals property. It ran from Mulberry Street on the south to Perry Place on the north. At one time, padlocked gates connecting the fences spanned North Line (Ford Avenue). Anyone wishing to enter Oakwood Cemetery had to request that the gates be opened.

Epilogue

With the annexation of Ford Village in 1922 and the area from 14th Street to Fort Street in 1924, Wyandotte reached its present boundaries. Growth and change would continue within these limits with each passing decade, but this photographic review stops here, after roughly the first 75 years of our city's history. We hope you have enjoyed this pictorial tour of Wyandotte's past!

Index

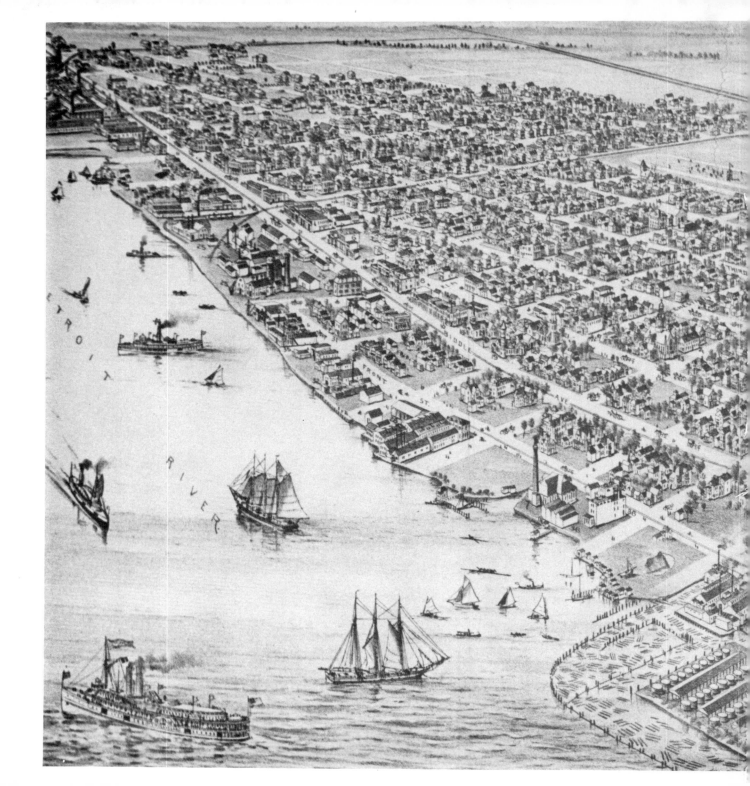